Work related neck
and upper limb
musculoskeletal
disorders

Report prepared by

Professor Peter Buckle and Dr. Jason Devereux
The Robens Centre for Health Ergonomics
European Institute of Health & Medical Sciences
University of Surrey
Guildford, Surrey, U.K
GU2 5XH

European Agency for
Safety and Health at
Work

A great deal of additional information on the European Union is available on the Internet.
It can be accessed through the Europa server (http://europa.eu.int).

Cataloguing data can be found at the end of this publication.

Luxembourg: Office for Official Publications of the European Communities, 1999

ISBN 92-828-8174-1

Printed in Belgium

FOREWORD

Following a request from the European Commission (DGV) and the approval by the Administrative Board the European Agency for Safety and Health at Work launched in May 1998 a research information project on "Work-related Upper Limb Disorders (WRULD)" in order to collect relevant research results and to describe and assess these findings. The scope of the study included the size of the problem within Member States of the European Union, the epidemiological evidence for causation by work, the pathological basis for work causation and intervention studies demonstrating the effectiveness of work system changes.

The European Agency invited the Robens Centre for Health Ergonomics, University of Surrey, U.K. to facilitate this work. This report on "Work-related Neck and Upper Limb Musculoskeletal Disorders" has been prepared by Professor Peter Buckle and Dr. Jason Devereux.

A special consultation process was carried out in the summer of 1999 by sending the manuscript to the members of the Thematic Network Group on Research - Work and Health, to DGV, to the European social partners and to other experts on the topic. After the consultation process the final report was prepared and published.

The European Agency wishes to thank the authors for their comprehensive work and all those individuals involved in the review process. We especially thank the participants who attended the expert meeting in Amsterdam during October 1998 who provided the foundation of the contents within the report.

Bilbao, 31 August 1999

European Agency for Safety and Health at Work

Contents

WORK-RELATED NECK AND UPPER LIMB MUSCULOSKELETAL DISORDERS - SUMMARY

Introduction

The European Commission (Directorate-General V) has requested the assistance of the European Agency for Safety and Health at Work to conduct a review of the available scientific knowledge regarding risk factors for work-related neck and upper limb musculoskeletal disorders (WRULDs). The European Agency invited Professor Peter Buckle and Dr. Jason Devereux of the Robens Centre for Health Ergonomics, University of Surrey, U.K. to facilitate this study and to prepare a report.

The report has drawn together knowledge from an extensive set of sources. These include the contemporary scientific literature, the views of an expert international scientific panel, current practice, employer and employee representatives and a number of official authorities from member states. The report is not a comprehensive review of all original research sources, but rather utilises authoritative reviews of such sources, where appropriate. Emphasis has been placed on those reviews that were agreed to be acceptable to the expert panel of scientists.

Assessment of work-related neck and upper limb musculoskeletal disorders (WRULDs)

There is little evidence of standardised criteria for use in the assessment of WRULDs across European Union (EU) member states. This is reflected in the nationally reported data as well as the research literature. Those studies that have reached consensus criteria for WRULDs assessments should be disseminated widely for further consultation, with a view to standardisation. However, it should be noted that the assessment criteria for primary preventative use in workplace surveillance and occupational health are different from the criteria used for some clinical interventions.

Size of the WRULDs problem

There is substantial evidence within the EU member states that neck and upper limb musculoskeletal disorders are a significant problem with respect to ill health and associated costs within the workplace. It is likely that the size of the problem will increase because workers are becoming more exposed to workplace risk factors for these disorders within the European Union.

Estimates of the cost of the WRULDs problem are limited. Where data do exist (e.g. the Nordic countries and the Netherlands) the cost has been estimated at between 0.5% and 2% of Gross National Product.

The lack of standardised assessment criteria for WRULDs makes comparison of data between member states difficult. In addition, little is known of the validity of the reported data. The true extent of ill health and associated costs within the workplace across member states is, therefore, difficult to assess. Despite this, studies that have used a similar design have reported large differences in prevalence rates between member states. The reasons for these differences require further investigation.

A number of epidemiological studies have found that women are at higher risk for work-related neck and upper limb musculoskeletal disorders, although associations with workplace risk factors are generally found to be stronger than gender factors. The importance of gender differences, and their implication for work system design, is largely outside the scope of this report but requires more substantial debate.

Biological mechanisms

Understanding of the biological mechanisms of WRULDs varies greatly with regard to the specific disorder in question. For carpal tunnel syndrome, for example, the body of knowledge is impressive, bringing together biomechanics, mathematical modelling and direct measurement of physiological and soft tissue changes. A coherent argument is provided from these sources that is persuasive of the biomechanically induced pathology of such disorders. For those disorders where the knowledge base is smaller, plausible hypotheses do exist and are currently the subject of much research interest.

Work-relatedness of WRULDs

The scientific reports, using defined criteria for causality, established a strong positive relationship between the occurrence of some WRULDs and the performance of work, especially where workers were highly exposed to workplace risk factors. Thus, the identification of workers in the extreme exposure categories should become a priority for any preventative strategy.

Consistently reported risk factors requiring consideration in the workplace are postural (notably relating to the shoulder and wrist), force applications at the hand, hand-arm exposure to vibration, direct mechanical pressure on body tissues, effects of a cold work environment, work organisation and worker perceptions of the work organisation (psychosocial work factors). The limited understanding of interactions between these variables means that the relationships describing the level of risk for varying amounts of exposure to risk factors in the workplace (i.e. exposure-response relationships) are difficult to deduce. However, those workers at high risk can be identified using current knowledge.

Scope for prevention

The report has not identified a specific form of action, however, it has provided a basis on which action could be formulated. The recommendations made are consistent with European directives on health and safety issues. The importance of a health and risk surveillance programme has been emphasised, and is supported by both existing European Union directives and a number of internationally recognised professional commissions and associations.

Many organisations have sought to implement ergonomic programmes and interventions aimed at primary prevention of WRULDs. This would suggest that they already believe in the effectiveness of ergonomic and occupational health strategies aimed at preventing the development of this group of disorders. They should be encouraged to help promote any further action. Organisations involved in prevention programmes are important role models for others. There is limited but persuasive evidence on the effectiveness of work system interventions incorporating ergonomics although the ability of organisations to implement the available ergonomics advice requires further consideration.

Appropriate ergonomics intervention on workplace risk factors for any single specific disorder is likely to help prevent other disorders. For example, reducing the exposure to hand-arm vibration will not only reduce the likelihood of the development of Raynaud's disease, but may also reduce the need for high force exertion at the hand and, thus, reduce the risk for hand/wrist tendinitis. Such benefits arise because of the common biological pathways involved in some of the disorders.

Scientists with experience of policy setting affirmed their belief that it was prudent to consider fatigue as a potential precursor to some of the disorders. Its use in surveillance programmes was also suggested. The role of fatigue is evident in some existing European health and safety directives and standards.

The report has considered the ability of those at the workplace (e.g. practitioners, worker representatives) to make risk assessments. Advice as to how such assessments could be made, given such restrictions, has been provided. The agreement of valid, standardised methods for the evaluation of working conditions and assessment of risk factors is required. The ergonomics work system approach must take due regard of the work risk factors identified in this report and a three level model of risk assessment has been proposed.

The report concludes that existing scientific knowledge could be used in the development of preventative strategies for WRULDs. These will be acceptable to many of those interested in prevention and are practical for implementation.

RESEARCH

and physical changes to the neck and upper limbs?

Does intervention in the workplace reduce the risks of work-related neck and upper limb musculoskeletal disorders?

What strategies are available to prevent work-related neck and upper limb musculoskeletal disorders?

It is important to recognise that this review was not intended to cover individual and other non-work factors and their relationship with neck and upper limb musculoskeletal disorders. It was not also intended to consider the role of clinical management, rehabilitation or return to work.

1.

INTRODUCTION

This report has addressed the following questions:

What is the extent of work-related neck upper limb musculoskeletal disorders within European member states?

What is the epidemiological evidence regarding work risk factors?

Is their coherent supporting evidence from the literature on underlying mechanisms

1.1

APPROACHES USED TO

PREPARE THE REPORT

This information has been collected from an expert meeting, literature review and consultation with further experts and interested parties.

Feedback has been sort on the initial draft of this report from approximately 40 individual experts, research groups and other organisations (available from the European Agency for Safety and Health at Work). Of the 20 responses, all but one has been wholly supportive of the general findings of the report. The exception requested an enlarged scope for the preventative measures in order to consider wider social systems interventions. The respondent's comments have, where feasible, been addressed in this final report.

1.1.1 Expert Meeting

The meeting of experts (see appendix 1 for membership of the panel) was held in Amsterdam, The Netherlands 7-11th October 1998. The aims of this meeting were to consider firstly whether there was agreement on the type and nature of neck and upper limb musculoskeletal disorders to be considered. Secondly, to review the data on the extent of neck and upper limb musculoskeletal disorders in the he workplace. Thirdly, whether there was sufficient evidence that these disorders are work related (considering both the epidemiological and pathogenic evidence). Fourthly, whether there was evidence that workplace interventions would reduce the risks associated with these disorders. Fifthly, to consider the optimal ergonomic approaches to prevention and finally whether further research studies were required. Each of these areas was considered during the four days in committee.

1.1.2 The Literature Search

The literature review has included obtained from the following sources:
- Scientific peer reviewed journals
- Conference proceedings
- Abstracts
- Recent textbooks
- Internally reviewed government or regulatory body reports
- CD ROM and online commercial and regulatory agency databases
- Bibliographies of recent and relevant articles
- Non-english literature articles considered relevant and translated into English
- Publisher on-line table of contents services for the latest research articles
- Reports not yet submitted or papers in press to scientific peer reviewed jour-

nals and provided by individual researchers.

The literature search has focused upon the following areas:
- Prevalence of disorders
- Epidemiology of disorders
- Mechanisms of disorders
- Intervention case studies and clinical case studies

The search terms have been included in the appendix 3.

Note: Although not included here, a full bibliography of sources is available.

1.1.3 Consultation and Liaison

Consultation and liaison with a number of established authorities or centres has also taken place (see appendix 2 for details). It is recognised that the opportunities and resources available for this process have been limited. It is hoped that wider consultation and more extensive views will be gathered following final publication of the report.

RESEARCH

the neck, shoulders, elbows, forearms, wrists and hands. The conditions for these regions are collectively referred to as the neck and upper limb musculoskeletal disorders (ULDs).

According to the World Health Organisation, work-related musculoskeletal disorders arise when exposed to work activities and work conditions that significantly contribute to their development or exacerbation but not acting as the sole determinant of causation (World Health Organization, 1985).

To give some indication of the specific conditions of neck and upper limb musculoskeletal disorders identified within the literature, Hagberg et al., (1995) have classified them according to whether a disorder is related to the tendon, nerve, muscle, circulation, joint or bursa. The disorders under each type are listed in table 1.

2.

THE NATURE OF

THE DISORDERS

The scientific committee for musculoskeletal disorders of the International Commission on Occupational Health (ICOH) recognise work-related musculoskeletal disorders which describe a wide range of inflammatory and degenerative diseases and disorders that result in pain and functional impairment (Kilbom et al., 1996).

Such conditions of pain and functional impairment may affect, besides others,

2.1

HOW ARE THE DISORDERS

MEASURED?

Clinical diagnostic criteria for health surveillance of these conditions across Europe are not yet available. Clinicians and researchers have relied upon different bodies of knowledge to justify the criteria used. However, general diagnostic criteria for work-related neck and upper limb disorders have been developed within individual member states, for example:

- UK – (Harrington et al., (1998), Cooper and Baker (1996))
- The Netherlands (Sluiter et al., (1998))
- Finland (Waris et al., (1979))
- Sweden (Ohlsson et al., (1994))
- Italy (Menoni et al., (1998))

The evaluation systems in each member state include a category for musculoskeletal conditions that are non-specific (i.e. where a specific diagnosis or pathology cannot be determined by physical examination but pain and/or discomfort is reported.) According to data sources in the U.K. approximately 50% of the cases that present with upper limb pain are classified as a non-specific upper limb conditions (Cooper and Baker, 1996).

Table 1. Classification of some neck and upper limb musculoskeletal disorders according to pathology. (Hagberg et al., 1995)

Tendon-related disorders	Nerve-related disorders	Muscle-related disorders	Circulatory/vascular type disorders	Joint-related disorders	Bursa-related disorders
Tendinitis/ peritendinitis/ tenosynovitis/ synovitis	Carpal tunnel syndrome	Tension neck syndrome	Hypothenar hammer syndrome	Osteoarthritis	Bursitis
Epicondylitis	Cubital tunnel syndrome	Muscle sprain and strain	Raynaud's syndrome		
De Quervain's disease	Guyon canal syndrome	Myalgia and myositis			
Dupuytren's contracture	Pronator teres syndrome				
Trigger finger	Radial tunnel syndrome				
Ganglion cyst	Thoracic outlet syndrome				
	Cervical syndrome				
	Digital neuritis				

Consultation with the expert panel has led to a detailed consideration of the need for specific and sensitive diagnostic criteria. Whilst the desirability of specific diagnostic criteria are recognised, the expert panel suggested that, in general, the prevention strategies recommended or put into practice to avoid the risks of these disorders would not be dependent upon the diagnostic classification. **It was also thought important that musculoskeletal disorders without a specific diagnosis or pathology be considered in health monitoring and surveillance systems.**

This conclusion is supported by a recent epidemiological study (Burdorf et al., 1998). The experience of symptoms of musculoskeletal disorders in the neck, shoulder and upper limbs has been shown to increase the risk of worker absence (recorded by the company) by approximately 2-4 times compared to workers not experiencing symptoms in a 2 year follow-up study.

The relationships between symptoms, injury reporting, impairment and disability remain unclear. A greater understanding of these relationships, along with the clinical natural history of these disorders would be beneficial (National Research Council, 1999).

2.2

HOW MANY EXPERIENCE

THESE DISORDERS

IN THE EU?

The prevalence rates of clinically verifiable neck and upper limb disorders using standardised diagnostic procedures across European member states are not currently available. However, surveys and injury reports to occupational health agencies have been used to estimate the size of the problem within Europe.

Evidence of the size of the problem can be derived from self-reports of musculoskeletal conditions across the European member states. Table 2 shows that the prevalence of self-reported symptoms of musculoskeletal disorders varies substantially between countries. Although such data are useful, the prevalence of self-reported symptoms may be under or overestimated in surveys because of methodological difficulties.

A programme in the Netherlands entitled "SAFE" commissioned a survey to collect information concerning the prevalence of work-related neck and upper limb disorders. In a study population of 10,813 employees in 1998, 30.5% had experienced self-reported neck and upper limbs in the previous 12 months (Blatter and Bongers, 1999). The study group was chosen to be representative of the Netherlands distribution of industrial sectors, company sizes and regions. However, a survey by the Central Bureau for Statistics in the Netherlands estimated that the prevalence of work-related complaints in the neck, shoulder, arm or wrists within the previous year in Dutch industry was approximately 19% in 1997 (Otlen et al., 1998).

Despite such differences, the approximate size of the problem can be appreciated by surveys, and each consistently shows that a substantial proportion of workers in the European Union experience work-related musculoskeletal conditions that affect the neck and upper limbs.

Further information is available in some member states[1], although definitions of both exposures and health outcomes are not standardised. This position has been recognised in a survey conducted by the European Trade Union Technical Bureau for Health and Safety (TUTB) in Brussels, Belgium (Tozzi, 1999). This showed that the information collected on musculoskeletal disorders by each EU member state was different in both definition and method of reporting. For these reasons it

---

[1] For example, the Spanish National Work Conditions Survey 1997, as supplied by the Instituto Nacional de Seguridad e Higiene en el Trabajo.

is not often possible to compare outcomes from different countries.

One study that has used a common approach is the Second European Survey on Working Conditions (Paoli, 1997). Figure 1 shows the percentage prevalence obtained for each member state. The size of the problem using this outcome meas-ure varies across each member state. However, in most the proportion of respondents reporting muscular pains in the arms and legs is considerable.

Some literature reflects the use of the International Classification of Disease-9th Revision (ICD-9). The accuracy of ICD-9 for identifying soft tissue disorders of the

Table 2. The prevalence of self-reported symptoms of musculoskeletal disorders within some EU member states.

Country	Study/ Organisation	Occupations	Prevalence	Outcome Definition
The Netherlands Belgium	TNO Work & Employment Amsterdam 1999 Blatter & Bongers 1999 Blatter et al., 1999	General Industry	30.5% 39.7%	Self-reported neck and upper limbs in the last 12 months
The Netherlands	POLS Population Survey Central Bureau for Statistics Otten et al., 1998	General industry	19%	Self-reported job related complaints of pain in the neck, shoulders, arm or wrist in the last year
2nd European Union Survey, Indicators of working conditions in the EU	European Foundation for the Improvement of Living and Woking Conditions, Dublin Paoli, 1997	General industry	17 %	Self-reported muscular pains in arms or legs affected by work
Great Britain	SWI The Health & Safety Executive Jones et al. 1998	General industry	17%	Self-reported symptoms in the neck and upper limbs in the last 12 months
Denmark	National Institute of Occupational Health Borg & Burr, 1997	General industry	29% of men, 46% of woman 26% of men, 44% of woman 14% of men, 20% of woman	Neck musculoskeletal problems Shoulders musc. problems Hands musc. problems (all in the last 12 months)
Sweden	The Working Environment Statistics Sweden, 1997 (Am 68 SM 9801)	General industry	Approximately 20% men Approximately 33% woman	Self-reported pain in the upper part of the back or neck, or in the shoulders or arms after work every week

neck and upper limbs has been studied (Buchbinder et al., 1996). Results show that the accuracy of ICD-9 is poor when compared to data taken from medical records.

Pilot data on recognised cases (classified according to the European Schedule of Occupational Diseases and collected by Eurostat) do not yet provide reliable estimates of the size of the problem. Different insurance systems and lists of prescribed diseases in the member states makes an accurate assessment of the size of the problem very unlikely.

Nevertheless, the data are available to enable suitable estimates on the nature, characteristics and trends of neck and upper limb musculoskeletal disorders to be made.

This view (TUTB, 1998) is also held by the European Trade Union Technical Bureau for Health and Safety (TUTB) and the European Trade Union Confederation (ETUC).

Some European member states have data from cases reported to national insurance and occupational health boards. In Sweden, for example, occupational injuries are reported to the National Board of Occupational Safety and Health. Diagnoses obtained in 1995 for work-related diseases of muscles, skeleton and other soft tissues for employed and self-employed workers totalled =9 398. Of these, 217 cases of rotator cuff tendonitis, 538 cases of epicondylitis, 215 cases of pain in the neck and 133 cases of pain in the neck and shoulders were identified (Broberg, 1997). Between 1990 and 1992 disorders of the musculoskeletal system (which include the lower limbs, back, neck, shoulders and upper limbs) represented at least 70% of all reports in Sweden. The prevalences of reported musculoskeletal disorders in Denmark and Finland were the largest of all reported occupational injuries (36% and 39% respectively). In Norway, musculoskeletal disorders constituted 15% of all reported occupational injuries (Broberg, 1996).

Table 3. Reported cases of occupational diseases by diagnosis in 1990-1992. The total number of cases N and the number of cases per 10 000 employed per year (freq).

	Denmark		Finland		Norway		Sweden	
	N	freq	N	freq	N	freq	N	freq
Carpal tunnel syndrome	456	0,6	90	0,1	6	-	1 288	1,1
Rotator cuff syndrome	633	0,8	6	-	145	0,3	3 350	2,9
Epicondylitis	-	-	4 224	6,0	23	-	6 614	5,7
Frozen shoulder	-	-	127	0,2	-	-	286	0,2
Synovitis, bursitis	7 142	9,1	5 286	7,6	389	0,7	1 571	1,4
Myalgia, myositis	2 141	2,7	22	-	171	0,3	12 773	11,0
Insertion tendinitis in hand/wrists	-	-	2	-	7	-	902	0,8
Unspecified vibration injury –Raynauds syndrome etc.	536	0,7	84	0,1	111	0,2	840	0,7

Source: (Broberg, 1996)

Table 3 shows of the size of the problem within the Nordic countries. The design of the workers' compensation systems in different countries probably influences the reporting behaviour and thereby the magnitude of the problems. There are also factors such as under/over-reporting and misclassification of reported diagnoses that affect comparisons between member states.

A significant proportion of all reported musculoskeletal diagnoses were considered to be associated with ergonomic work risk factors – Norway 15%, Denmark and Finland 40% and Sweden 70% (Broberg, 1996).

In Italy, musculoskeletal disorders, other than vibration white finger, have only been compensated in the last 2-3 years. According to the management of the National Institute for Insurance of Injuries and Occupational Diseases, the claims for musculoskeletal disorders have been increasing strongly in this period. Musculoskeletal disorders from biomechanical overload increased from 873 reports in 1996 to 2000 in 1999.

In 1998, 60% of claims for musculoskeletal disorders in the upper limbs were recognised as occupational diseases and so resulted in compensation. More than 60% of the conditions were carpal tunnel syndrome and the remainder was tendinitis and tenosynovitis of the hand and wrist, and epicondylitis of the elbow[2].

These musculoskeletal conditions are not included in the official list of occupational diseases in Italy but, following a high court ruling in 1979, it is possible to compensate workers if it can be demonstrated that a clear exposure-response relationship for a specific disorder exists (Bovenzi, 1999).

Between 1988-1998 in Italy, there were 5360 cases compensated for vibration-induced disorders of the upper limbs with a maximum number of cases (n=863) in 1991 and a minimum in 1998 (n=169). In the same decade, vibration-induced disorders as a percentage of all compensated occupational diseases ranged between 3.9% and 5% per year. The percentage of compensated cases for vibration-induced disorders of the upper limbs tends to remain stable. There is a general tendency towards a comparable reduction in the number of compensated cases for vibration-induced disorders and the total number of compensated occupational diseases.

According to the Institut National de Recherche et de Sécurité (INRS) in France, the percentage of recognised and compensated musculoskeletal disorders compared to the total number of occupational ill health diseases has steadily increased from 40% (n=2,602) in 1992 to 63% (n=5,856) in 1996.

In Great Britain, a labour force survey conducted by the Health and Safety Executive estimated that 506 000 workers experienced a self-reported condition that affected the neck or upper limbs in 1995. The types of disorders reported included

---

[2]   Data kindly provided by Dr. Bovenzi, University of Trieste, Italy and Prof. Grieco, University of Milan, Italy.

carpal tunnel syndrome, frozen shoulder, tenosynovitis, tennis or golfer's elbow and RSI. Limitation of movement was reported by 86% of the survey respondents (Jones et al., 1998). As a result of the number of workers experiencing these conditions, approximately 5.5 million working days were lost annually due to musculoskeletal disorders of the neck and the upper limbs and, in addition, 110 000 working days were lost annually due to vibration white finger, according to the survey (Jones et al., 1998). The number of days lost annually for neck and upper limb musculoskeletal disorders was equivalent to the number for back disorders.

Extrapolation from a survey of general practitioners in Britain suggests that 20 000 cases of work-related carpal tunnel syndrome occur per year. This disorder was either caused or exacerbated by work or interfered with the ability to work. This represents approximately half of the number of cases with carpal tunnel syndrome seen by those doctors that responded to the survey (Health and Safety Commission, 1995).

In Great Britain, data are collected on the number of assessed cases of disablement for a range of upper limb musculoskeletal disorders that result in benefit paid (severe disablement) or unpaid. The assessed conditions include beat hand, beat elbow, tenosynovitis, vibration white finger and carpal tunnel syndrome. The data indicate that the number of claims resulting in benefit compared to the total number of assessed claims has risen from 1.7% in 1990 to 22.5% (n=949) in 1996/97.

Therefore, the number of claims that have resulted in disablement benefits has increased while the number of claims for upper limb musculoskeletal disorders resulting in no benefits has decreased (Health and Safety Commission, 1998). Of all the prescribed industrial disease claims (that included physical, biological and chemical agents) in 1996/7 that resulted in benefits, approximately 62% were due to upper limb musculoskeletal disorders. The total number of claims assessed for upper limb musculoskeletal disorders was 4220. In comparison, the total number of claims assessed for occupational deafness was 413 (approximately 1/10th of the 4220 cases of ULDs). The perception in the U.K, however, is that there is a much higher increase in work-related upper limb disorders that are presented to medical experts and dealt with through the legal system and which are not prescribed industrial diseases (Helliwell, 1996).

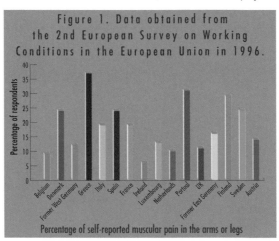

Figure 1. Data obtained from the 2nd European Survey on Working Conditions in the European Union in 1996.

Percentage of self-reported muscular pain in the arms or legs

2.3

THE COST OF THE PROBLEMS

was approximately 0.5-2% of the gross national products in the Nordic countries (Data from Morch, 1996; Hansen and Jensen, 1993.)

In Britain, the Health and Safety Executive (HSE) estimated that work-related upper limb disorders incurred approximate costs of £1.25 billion per year (Davies and Teasdale, 1994).

The direct costs from compensation of musculoskeletal disorders are appreciated far more than the indirect costs associated with disruptions in productivity and quality, worker replacement costs, training and work absence costs. It is believed that the direct costs due to compensated work related musculoskeletal disorders are only a relatively low proportion (30-50%) of the total costs (Hagberg et al., 1995). Borghouts et al. (1999) have estimated that the direct costs of neck pain in the Netherlands for 1996 were $160 million dollars and the indirect costs were $527 million. The total cost of neck pain represented 0.1% of the gross domestic product in 1996.

Not every European member state collects information on the costs of neck and upper limb musculoskeletal disorders. Toomingas (1998)[3] estimated that about 20-25% of all expenditure for medical care, sick leave and sickness pensions in the Nordic countries in 1991 was related to conditions of the musculoskeletal system, of which 20-80% were work related.

Half of these conditions were attributed to neck and upper limb musculoskeletal disorders and, in Sweden, these problems constituted 15% of all sick-leave days and 18% of all sickness pensions in 1994 (Statistics Sweden, 1997).

Estimates by Toomingas (1998) have shown that the total expenditure for neck and upper limb musculoskeletal disorders

There is substantial evidence to suggest that neck and upper limb musculoskeletal disorders are a significant problem within the European Union. Some member states have identified a major ill-health and financial burden associated with these problems.

---

[3] Estimate based on "Working environment and national economies in the Nordic Countries" by the Nordic Council of Ministers (Report No. 556, 1993 by Hansen,M. and Jensen,P.)

2.3.1 Research Priorities

Survey results from the Netherlands and the U.K. have identified a priority need for research in the topic of work-related upper limb musculoskeletal disorders.

The research priority needs in the Netherlands were assessed by surveying the occupational health and safety services, scientific research institutions, government and companies (Van der Beek et al., 1997). It was collectively decided that preventive measures and control solutions were the highest priority area in order to improve work conditions.

Two surveys conducted in the U.K. by the Institute of Occupational Health (University of Birmingham) provided information regarding the priorities in research according to occupational physicians and personnel managers (Harrington, 1994; Harrington and Calvert, 1996). Both occupational groups acknowledged back, neck and upper limb musculoskeletal disorders as an outcome that needed priority research but personnel managers considered practical strategies more important than risk factor identification, which was the reverse view of the physicians.

Trade union initiatives in EU member states have shown increasing employer awareness regarding musculoskeletal disorders. A need to increase this awareness has been identified according to surveys conducted by trade unions in France, Spain, the United Kingdom and Denmark (TUTB, 1996).

This review suggests that neck and upper limb musculoskeletal disorders are increasingly recognised as a significant occupational health problem by occupational doctors, employers, academia, trade unions and governments. There are data that support the need to address these disorders within the European Union.

2.4

SCIENTIFIC BASIS FOR

PREVENTION

Ergonomic interventions may reduce the occurrence by approximately 30-40% (Hansen and Jensen, 1993). This is based upon the number of musculoskeletal disorders cases considered to be work related in the Nordic countries. For occupations that are highly exposed to work risk factors for musculoskeletal problems the proportion may be as high as 50-90% (Hagberg and Wegman, 1987).

The expert panel suggested that one preventative strategy might commence by identifying groups that are highly exposed to risk factors for neck and upper limb musculoskeletal disorders. They considered that the greatest benefits, relative to the resources required, might be realised by reducing the risks in these groups.

2.4.1 Industries at risk

Data from the 2nd European Survey on Working Conditions (Paoli, 1997) identified the industries (across the European member states) where 40% or more of the workers were exposed to three or more of the following risk factors for at least 25% of the working time:

- Working in painful positions
- Moving heavy loads
- Short repetitive tasks
- Repetitive movements

The industries where the greatest exposures were identified included:

- Agriculture, forestry and fisheries
- Mining, manufacturing
- Construction
- Wholesale, retail and repairs
- Hotels and restaurants

High exposures were also found in other industries.

The occupational groups with the greatest exposures were agriculture and fishery workers, craft and retail trade workers, plant and machine operators and workers in elementary occupations.

The industries with the least exposure to these risk factors included:

- Transport and communication
- Financial and intermediation
- Real estate and business activity
- Public administration

In the Netherlands (Blatter and Bongers, 1999), some of the highest annual prevalence rates of work related neck and upper limb symptoms have been found in the industries that are the most highly exposed to the risk factors for neck and upper limb musculoskeletal disorders and include:

- Hotel, restaurant and catering (40%)
- Construction (38%)
- Production (33%)

2.4.2 Occupations at Risk

Tailors (47%), building construction workers (43%), loaders/unloaders (42%), secretaries and typists (38%) were some of the occupations with the highest annual prevalences of symptoms. This compared to the lowest prevalence found for commercial occupations (21%). These data came from a study in the Netherlands of 10,813 employees and used self-reported work-related neck and upper limb symptoms (Blatter and Bongers, 1999).

The Second European Survey (Paoli, 1997) found that the occupational groups with the least exposures were legislators and managers, professionals, technicians and clerks. It is important to note that industrial sector or occupational classifications may be misleading when identifying areas requiring priority action. This is because a job title may consist of a wide range of job tasks associated with risks, and the duration and distribution of these tasks may vary considerably between each worker (Kauppinen, 1994). It has been shown that these data can be used to form broad categories of jobs with similar exposure to work demands (de Zwart et al., 1997). These may provide informative patterns of work related disorders. Therefore, it is important to assess each job that is performed rather than rely on crude estimates of risk for industrial sectors or occupational groups.

Not only are many workers in the European Union highly exposed to work risk factors for neck and upper limb musculoskeletal disorders but the magnitude of the exposure seems to be increasing, according to research by the European Foundation for the Improvement of Living and Working Conditions, Dublin, Ireland (Dhondt and Houtman,1997).

In the four years between the first and second European Surveys on Working Conditions in Europe, the percentage of workers exposed for greater than 50% of the working time increased for the following:

- Working in painful postures
- Handling heavy loads
- Working at high speed
- Working with deadlines

It would seem, therefore, that there is considerable potential for reducing the exposure to work related risk factors of neck and upper limb musculoskeletal disorders.

2.4.3 Gender as a risk factor

A number of epidemiological studies have found that women are at higher risk for work related neck and upper limb disorders (e.g. Hagberg and Wegman, 1987), whilst other studies report no such differences (e.g. Silverstein, 1985). Comparisons between work and gender factors frequently find stronger associations with workplace risk factors (Burt, 1998). Other factors thought to be important in understanding the observed gender differences are that females are often employed in more hand intensive tasks and that anthropometric differences (e.g. body size, strength) might disadvantage the female worker in work systems where no consideration has been taken of such differences (Nordander et al., 1999). This might apply, in particular, to tool design (Pheasant, 1991, 1996) and work surface heights. The importance of gender differences is largely outside the scope of this report but requires more substantial debate.

2.5

SUMMARY - THE NATURE

OF THE DISORDERS

There is substantial evidence within the EU member states that neck and upper limb musculoskeletal disorders are a significant problem with respect to ill health and associated costs within the workplace.

There are few estimates of the cost of these problems. Where data do exist (e.g. Nordic countries) the cost has been estimated at between 0.5% and 2% of GNP. It is likely that the size of the problem will increase as exposure to work-related risk factors for these conditions is increasing within the European Union.

A number of member states (e.g. Sweden, Great Britain) have studied representative samples of the workforce with regard to the site of musculoskeletal disorders. Results have shown that problems for the neck and upper limb are second in importance only to back disorders, as judged through self-reported symptom prevalence.

There is little evidence of the use of standardised criteria across member states. This is reflected in the nationally reported data as well as the research literature and makes comparison between member states difficult. Studies that have reached consensus diagnostic criteria should be disseminated widely for further consultation, with a view to standardisation. This report recognises that the criteria for primary preventative use in workplace surveillance and occupational health will be different from the criteria used for some clinical interventions.

Those studies that have used the same methodological criteria have reported large differences in prevalence rates between member states. The reasons for this require further investigation.

A number of epidemiological studies have found that women are at higher risk for work related neck and upper limb disorders, although associations with workplace risk factors are generally found to be stronger than gender factors. The importance of gender differences, and their implication for work system design, is largely outside the scope of this report but requires more substantial debate.

RESEARCH

3.

THE RELATIONSHIP BETWEEN

WORK AND NECK AND UPPER

LIMB DISORDERS

3.1

MODELS FOR THE

PATHOGENESIS OF THE

DISORDERS

Researchers from Denmark, Finland, Sweden, England and the United States developed a conceptual model to promote the understanding of the possible pathways that could lead to the development of neck and upper limb musculoskeletal disorders (Armstrong et al., 1993).

This model, shown in figure 2, describes four sets of interacting concepts - exposure, dose, capacity and response. Worker activity produces internal forces acting upon the tissues

of the body over time (termed a dose). The dose causes effects such as increased circulation, local muscle fatigue and other various physiological and biomechanical effects i.e. there is a response by the body initiated by internal stimuli, which themselves arise from external factors. The response of the body may increase or decrease the ability to maintain or improve the capacity to cope with further responses.

Over time, a reduced capacity may affect the dose and the subsequent response. To clarify, if there if insufficient time to allow the capacity of the tissues to regenerate then a further series of responses is likely to further degenerate the available capacity. This may continue until some type of structural tissue deformation occurs that may be experienced, for example, as pain, swelling or limited movement.

Whilst this model is useful for explaining the cumulative nature of neck and upper limb musculoskeletal disorders, it was recognised by the experts that there are alternative pathways not considered in this model. Other models (Van der Beek and Frings-Dresen, 1998; Winkel and Mathiassen, 1994) suggest that a pathway between work capacity and

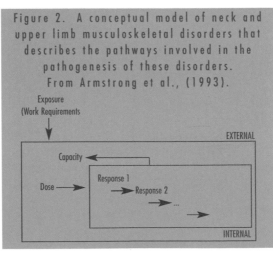

Figure 2. A conceptual model of neck and upper limb musculoskeletal disorders that describes the pathways involved in the pathogenesis of these disorders. From Armstrong et al., (1993).

the work activity may exist, such that a reduction in capacity may result in a reduction in the amount of work performed. This reduction in work activity may be sufficient to allow worker capacity to increase.

The concept of exposure in figure 2 can be expanded to include the model proposed by Dutch researchers (Van der Beek and Frings-Dresen, 1998). Figure 3, therefore, shows the exposure or work requirements operationalised as the working situation, the actual working method, and posture, movements and exerted forces.

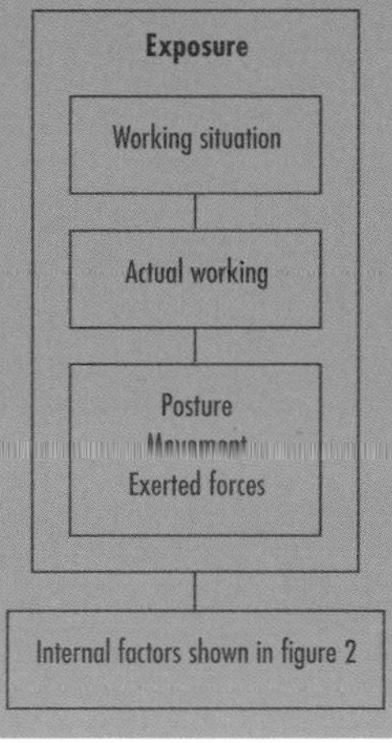

The working situation is characterised by work demands and job decision latitude. The latter is defined as the extent of autonomy and opportunities for workers to improve (or to make worse) the working situation by altering the work demands. The working situation is, therefore, characterised by the organisation of work (work organisation factors) and the perceptions held by workers regarding the way the work is organised (psychosocial work factors).

The working situation constructs the way a worker performs the work activity. This can be affected by individual characteristics such as anthropometry, physical fitness, age, gender, and previous medical history.

The method that an individual worker adopts will affect the level, duration and frequency of exposure to work postures, executed movements and the forces exerted. This will affect the internal factors previously discussed (see figure 2.)

The model shown in figure 4 (National Research Council, 1999) provides additional concepts for those factors that lie external to the individual (i.e. those that comprise exposure in the Armstrong et al. (1993) model). Whilst not all of these factors are considered within this report, it was considered appropriate to provide a broader view that showed the potential importance of factors such as non-work activities and individual factors. Work organisation, production rates and the time taken to perform a work task affect the frequency and duration of force exertions. In some instances, the time taken for a process change can determine soft tissue recovery times. The postures adopted in the workplace are affected by the design of work equipment, the location of objects, the size and shape of handles and the orientation of objects.

Figure 3. Expansion of the exposure box shown in figure 2. Adapted from Van der Beek and Frings-Dresen (1998).

In conclusion, the three models show considerable agreement. They serve as a useful basis for exploring research hypotheses. They also provide a framework for understanding both the pathogenesis and the relationship of these disorders with work.

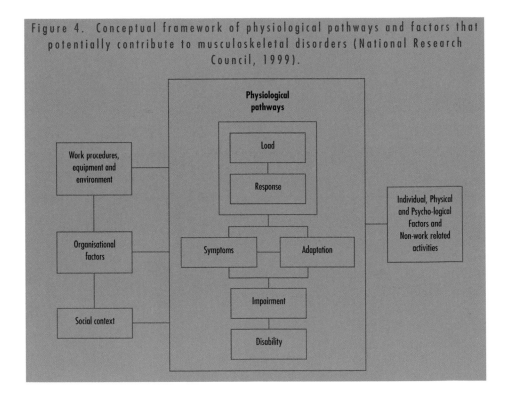

Figure 4. Conceptual framework of physiological pathways and factors that potentially contribute to musculoskeletal disorders (National Research Council, 1999).

3.2

BIOLOGICAL RESPONSES

AND PATHOLOGY

The 1999 National Research Council review provides a contemporary and authoritative overview of the response of soft tissue to physical stressors encountered during work system practices (National Research Council, 1999). It has highlighted the importance of considering the biological responses of tissues to biomechanical stressors. The expert panel involved in this report did not feel that there was one single common pathway for all exposures although the importance of the biomechanical pathway was recognised.

It has been shown that activities at work, daily living and recreation may often produce biomechanical loads upon the body that approach the limits of the mechanical properties of soft tissues. Up to certain limits some types of soft tissue, like mus-

cle, adapt to repetitive loading while other tissue such as nerves are less adaptable.

The expert panel was of the opinion that the biomechanical stressors needed to be considered in conjunction with individual factors, the concept of internal loads and responses to internal loads (see Armstrong et al., 1993) and non-biomechanical factors (e.g. work organisational, social and other psychological factors).

All soft tissues including muscles, tendons, fascia, synovia and the nerve will fail when sufficient force is applied (National Research Council, 1999). Ethical issues in experimental research prevent many such studies from having been performed with in-vivo human tissue. However, cadaver studies and animal modelling have provided supportive evidence of the limits for such tissues before failure occurs. The tissue response may be in the form of deformation leading to inflammation, muscle fatigue and failure at a microscopic level.

The extent to which the tissues fail with regard to single event, cumulative or repetitive action has also been documented in a number of studies. The National Research Council (1999) review considers these and also describes how these findings can be applied to humans in the workplace. It notes that the laboratory studies meet the causal criteria laid down with regard to: temporal ordering, cause and effect covariation, the absence of other plausible explanations for the observed effect, temporal contiguity; and congruity between the cause and effect.

The following section provides examples of how each of the soft tissues at risk in the neck and upper limb has been considered with regard to the responses and fatigue/failure that may occur. It is not intended to be a comprehensive overview of the area, but rather is intended to demonstrate that there is suitable documented scientific literature that allows us to establish that mechanisms can and do exist, whilst also acknowledging that some aspects require further research. It should be appreciated that an holistic understanding of the full pathogenesis of each disorder is not yet available. However, where mechanisms have yet to be determined, plausible hypotheses have been developed and are being tested.

Recent reviews by Ashton-Miller (1999), Hägg (1998), Rempel et al., (1999), Radwin and Lavender (1999) and Winkel and Westgaard (1992) have proved especially helpful in preparing this section.

3.2.1 Muscle pathology

Hägg (1998) has reviewed the literature regarding muscle fibre abnormalities in the upper trapezius muscle with respect to occupational static load and work related myalgia in the shoulder/neck region. This is a common complaint in workers exposed to high static or repetitive load in the shoulder region. The review recognises that the underlying physiological mechanisms causing this myalgia are only partially understood.

Early hypotheses suggested that general ischemia due to high static load with the resultant occlusion or impedance of circulation was a causative factor (Jonsson, 1982). However, later research by Veiersted et al. (1993) has shown that problems of myalgia can occur at very low contraction levels. This, and other research, led Hägg (1991) to the hypothesis that specific muscle fibres or motor units may be selectively affected. This could result from patterns of recruitment. It is also evident that some aspects of psychological stress can cause additional static load on the trapezius muscle (Waersted and Westgaard, 1996; Melin and Lundberg, 1997). Methodological difficulties exist in taking muscle fibre from human subjects. For ethical reasons, the number of samples that can be taken and the size of such samples is extremely limited. There is evidence of change in characteristics of the fibres in those exposed to high repetitive and static workload compared to those who have not been exposed to these factors. The irregularities observed appear to be related to the fibre mitochondria. Hägg (1998) suggests that mitochondrial disturbances are a result of static and/or repetitive workload in the upper trapezius muscle.

However, the research does not determine whether the disturbances lead necessarily to myalgia. The relationship between abnormality in muscle fibre and the subsequent perception of pain by subjects requires further study. Hägg (1998) has indicated that these types of muscle abnormalities may be a necessary but not sufficient condition for pain perception. Of further interest, is the observation that type I muscle fibres show mitochondrial disturbances - type I fibres being those that are recruited first when static loads are exerted.

Hagberg et al. (1995) have considered the potential role of impact loads on upper limb disorders. It is recognised that those who, in the course of their work, use the hand as a hammer have the potential to cause vascular disorders. Similarly, eccentric contractions are recognised as having a high potential for muscle damage (Edwards, 1988). These have been considered further by Ashton-Miller (1999). Such rapid eccentric contractions of muscles may be seen to occur when the worker absorbs the "kick-back" or torque on powered tools, such as screwdrivers.

3.2.2 Tendon/ligament

Tendons, mainly formed of collagenous tissue, provide a link between muscle and bone. Under some conditions of repeated loading the tendons may become inflamed. This seems to occur especially where the tendons are loaded both by tensile forces (generated by or transferred to the muscle) and in a transverse direction by reaction forces (Armstrong et al., 1984). This seems most likely to occur when the tendons pass over adjacent soft and hard structures (e.g. bony structures) especially in awkward postures or at end of range of motion. Friction between the tendon and adjacent surfaces may also lead to degeneration of the surface of the tendon. Chaffin and Andersson (1991) have noted that in some instances collagen fibres become separated. The resultant changes can cause swelling and pain. The same authors have considered the biomechanics of the tendon and the prob-

able changes that would occur should the supporting synovia become inflamed. The resultant changing coefficient of friction has given rise to the concept that repeated compression would then further aggravate synovial inflammation and swelling.

Experimental studies (e.g. Backman et al, 1990) have provided evidence that repetitive loading of the tendon can induce histological changes. Further study is required of the characteristics of mechanical loading and how they cause tendon dysfunction including preventing healing and adequate remodelling. Studies are also required in order to investigate the potential for slowed healing. Cumulative micro-strain is considered a plausible hypothesis for tendon/ligament injury in upper limb disorders (e.g. Goldstein et al., 1987).

3.2.3 Nerve

Elevated pressures around the nerve can inhibit intraneural, microvascular flow, axonal transport, nerve function and cause endoneurial oedema with increased intrafascicular pressure and displacement of myelin in a dose-response manner Rempel et al. (1998). Such effects can occur within minutes or hours. Viikari-Juntura and Silverstein (1999) state that acute effects on the nerve are usually followed by rapid recovery but prolonged or very high pressure can result in irreversible effects. In one animal model, extraneural pressures of 4kPa applied for two hours initiated a process of nerve injury and repair. It also was shown to cause structural tissue changes, which persisted for one month. Rempel et al. (1998) point out that whilst a dose-response relationship with pressure occurs, the critical pressure/duration values for nerve injury are unknown. It is known that in healthy humans, non-neutral wrist and forearm postures and force exertion at the fingertips can elevate extraneural pressure in the carpal tunnel in a dose-response manner. Such pressures are consistent with the level at which intraneural microvascular blood flow may become affected.

Exposure to vibrating hand tools at work can lead to permanent nerve injury. The pathophysiological process associated with a neuropathy induced by vibration is not fully understood, but animal models have been developed which evaluate the events taking place in peripheral nerves following vibration exposure. Changes noticed include intraneural oedema, structural changes in myelinated and unmyelinated fibres in the nerve, as well as functional changes of both the nerve fibres and non-neuronal cells.

Strömberg et al. (1997) have considered the structural nerve changes at wrist level in workers when exposed to vibration. They show severe nerve injury at the dorsal interosseous nerve just proximal to the wrist. This and other studies have shown that long term use of hand held vibrating tools can induce changes in peripheral circulation such as white fingers, as well as sensory disturbances and muscle weakness (Brammer et al., 1987; Pyykkö, 1986). In animal models, structural changes have been reported in the myelinated and unmyelinated nerve fibres after exposure to vibration. Finger biopsies from patients with vibration induced white fingers show changes in the nerve fibres as well as in the connective tissue components of peripheral nerves (Strömberg et al., 1997). Their findings suggest that such pathology may occur in the carpal tunnel following exposure to vibration. They identify two possible pathogenic mechanisms in carpal tunnel syndrome in those exposed to vibration. The first being nerve compression and the other being changes introduced by vibration itself.

Plausible hypotheses, such as these, are common in the literature. It is also important to consider exposure to several factors simultaneously. The interactions between the soft tissues and the subsequent effects of the interactions are still only partially understood.

3.2.4 Circulation

Circulatory changes following exposure to hand arm vibration or varying frequency and acceleration magnitudes. Recent studies (e.g. Bovenzi et al., 1998) would suggest that, in addition, the duration of exposure contributes to the reaction of the digital vessels to acute vibration. Some studies (e.g. Egan et al, 1996) suggest that a central vasomotor mechanism may be involved in the immediate response of finger circulation to vibration exposure.

3.2.5 Local Mechanical Pressure

Hagberg et al. (1995) have considered the possible relationship between local mechanical pressure and the onset of musculoskeletal problems. Direct mechanical pressures on tissues can occur with, for example, poorly designed tools and handles. Thus, pressure from metal tools, such as scissors can lead to digital neuritis and there are a number of vulnerable sites in the palm of the hand. Sauter et al. (1987) have also considered the potential pressures on the wrist from supporting weights. Buckle (1994) has reviewed the potential neurological outcomes of such mechanical pressures including the carrying of loads. Others (e.g. Fransson-Hall and Kilbom, 1993) have considered other effects of direct mechanical pressure.

3.2.6 Cold

Hagberg et al., (1995) evaluated cold as a risk factor. Cold may act directly as a risk factor for neck and upper limb musculoskeletal disorders. Alternatively, it may act indirectly or a result of the additional problems for the worker that arise when wearing personal protective equipment. Difficulties in researching this issue are evident. For example, Chiang et al. (1990) identified cold as a risk factor for carpal tunnel syndrome, however all the subjects working in cold environment were also wearing gloves. Others, for example Vincent and Tipton (1988), have found reductions in maximum grip strength of 13-18% following immersion in cold water. Such findings suggest that the physiological demands on muscle and related tissues will be greater in a cold environment for any given work task. Increased muscle activity, as observed by Sunderlin and Hagberg (1992), may arise from direct cooling of tissue or postural changes, designed to be protective from the cold.

3.2.7 Pain sensitisation

Muscle pain is the most common symptom of musculoskeletal disorders (Sjøgaard, 1990). Painful and nonpainful chemical stimulii from a musculoskeletal disorder may increase the sensitivity of the injured tissues. This phenomenon, referred to as sensitisation (Blair, 1996; Besson, 1999), has been observed in clinical cases that experience persistent symptoms and ongoing musculoskeletal problems.

Levine et al. (1985) have reported that musculoskeletal trauma or repetitive motion may produce painful and nonpainful stimulii that generate a release of adrenergic chemicals from sympathetic nerve fibres. These chemicals affect joints, muscle spindles, primary C-fibres and the muscle itself.

In the joints, for example, a chain reaction of chemicals is initiated as a direct effect of the activation of the postganglionic sympathetic fibres. Norepinephrine, discharged from the fibres, will affect smooth muscle and secretory, lymphoid and inflammatory cells. Blair (1996) and Besson (1999) believe that this triggers the release of several inflammatory mediators such as bradykinin, prostaglandins, serotonine, histamine, substance P, neurokinin A that activate the C-fibre nociceptor, one type of the peripheral nerves that carry pain signals to the central nervous system.

The nerve endings become more sensitive with the continued release of inflammatory mediators and this lowers the threshold for stimulation i.e. smaller external loads to the injured area result in spontaneous pain (Blair, 1996). With chronic pain syndrome, the intensity of pain is frequently out of proportion to the original injury or tissue damage (Loeser and Melzack, 1999).

A model proposed by Johansson and Sojka (1991) implied that sustained muscle contractions, inflammation, and/or ischaemia could begin a 'vicious circle' of muscle stiffness to primary and secondary muscles and thereby preserve or increase the production of metabolites and the high activity in the chemosensitive nerve endings. The model has been used to explain the observation that muscle tension and pain tend to propagate from one muscle to surrounding muscles in many chronic musculoskeletal pain syndromes. Research, for example (Djupsjöbacka et al., 1995; Pedersen et al., 1997; Wenngren et al., 1998) has supported this model. In addition, Bergenheim et al. (1995) have noted an additional pathway where contraction metabolites and inflammatory substances may alter muscle coordination, thus, increasing the load on active muscle motor units. Increased muscle activity (i.e. highly active muscle motor units) measured using electromyography during stereotyped tasks in workers with pain and/or chronic pain (e.g. myalgia) has been demonstrated (Veierstad et al., 1990).

3.3

THE EPIDEMIOLOGICAL

EVIDENCE OF WORK-

RELATEDNESS

The National Institute of Occupational Safety and Health (NIOSH), U.S.A., have critically reviewed the epidemiological evidence for work-related musculoskeletal disorders, including the neck and upper limbs (NIOSH, 1997).

Work related physical risk factors were identified for the neck/shoulders, shoulder region, elbows and hands/wrists (see table 4).

The epidemiological studies for each type of musculoskeletal disorder were summarised with regard to determinants of causality that included:

- Strength of the association between work exposure and musculoskeletal outcome
- The consistency of the association across studies
- The temporal effect between becoming exposed and developing the disorder(s)

- Evidence of an exposure-response relationship
- Coherence of the epidemiological evidence with respect to other types of scientific evidence e.g. laboratory studies

Table 4 shows that there is consistent epidemiological evidence supporting the work-relatedness of many musculoskeletal disorders of the neck and upper limbs. The report also concluded that high levels of exposure, especially in combination with exposure to more than one physical factor provided the strongest evidence of work relatedness for these disorders. In addition, the strongest evidence came from studies in which workers were exposed daily and for whole-shifts.

It was acknowledged that individual factors (e.g. previous medical history) may influence the degree of risk from specific exposures and it is likely that the reviewed disorders may also be caused by non-work factors. This did not substantially alter the association with work factors.

Psychosocial work factors were considered within the NIOSH review and, despite the evidence not being entirely consistent, it was concluded that intensified workload, low job control, low social support and perceived monotonous work may be involved in the development of work-related upper limb disorders.

A more recent review of the evidence has been prepared by a scientific steering committee and scientists (National Research Council, 1999). This review, approved by the Governing board of the National Research Council, U.S.A., exam-

Table 4. The work relatedness of musculoskeletal disorders:
Physical work risk factors. Source: NIOSH, (1997).

Body part Risk factor	Strong evidence	Evidence	Insufficient evidence	Evidence of no effect
Neck and Neck/shoulder				
Repetition		✔		
Force		✔		
Posture	✔			
Vibration			✔	
Shoulder				
Repetition		✔		
Force			✔	
Posture		✔		
Vibration			✔	
Elbow				
Repetition			✔	
Force		✔		
Posture			✔	
Combination	✔			
Hand/wrist				
Carpal tunnel syndrome				
Repetition		✔		
Force		✔		
Posture			✔	
Vibration		✔		
Combination	✔			
Tendinitis				
Repetition		✔		
Force		✔		
Posture		✔		
Combination	✔			
Hand-armvibration syndrome				
Vibration	✔			

ined the current state of the scientific research base. It considered the epidemiological evidence as well as the potential biological mechanisms and the evidence from effective interventions

The review concluded that there was a positive relationship between the occurrence of musculoskeletal disorders (back, neck and upper limbs) and the performance of work, when considering the highest levels of exposure to biomechanical work factors and the sharpest contrasts in exposure among study groups.

There was compelling evidence that a reduction in the biomechanical load results in a reduction in the prevalence of musculoskeletal disorders. This evidence further supports the relationship between work activities and the occurrence of musculoskeletal disorders.

There was less definitive evidence that low levels of biomechanical stressors are associated with musculoskeletal disorders, although there are some high quality studies suggesting causal associations that should serve as a basis for further research. Where low levels of biomechanical stress are experienced it was thought important to consider also the possible contribution of other factors to musculoskeletal disorders (e.g. social and organisational factors).

This study also found that a more rigorous elimination of studies in the earlier NIOSH review would not have substantially altered the conclusions that had been reached.

Individual, organisational and social factors were characterised. It was recognised that individuals differ in their susceptibility to the incidence, severity and aetiology of musculoskeletal disorders. Age and prior medical history are two individual factors that have biological plausibility to account for the strong relationships observed in epidemiological studies.

Organisational and social factors have been referred to under one term known as psychosocial work factors. These are factors directly associated with levels of workplace stress such as job content and demands, job control and social support. In general, reviews in the scientific literature have shown that poor job content (poor task integration and lack of task identity) and high job demands were related to musculoskeletal disorders. In theory, these factors may act biologically through increased biomechanical strain, physiolog-

ical vulnerability, or symptom attribution and reporting. It was considered that psychosocial factors had a moderate effect on the impact of work-related musculoskeletal disorders (National Research Council, 1999).

Despite a lack of standardised methods, the resultant variability enabled the examination of a common set of musculoskeletal conditions from a multiple perspective. This was considered to strengthen the causal inferences made.

It was noted that the time order between being exposed to the physical work factors and the development of musculoskeletal disorders (or the clinical course) was less consistently demonstrated.

Finally, the relative contribution of work related factors to the incidence or prevalence of musculoskeletal disorders in the general population could not be considered because of scarce evidence.

Researchers (Grieco et al., 1998) at the University of Milan, Italy compared the results from the NIOSH review (1997) with the review of the work relatedness of neck and upper limb musculoskeletal by Hagberg et al. (1995). They also considered the biological plausibility of the associations between work and the disorders. They concluded that there was satisfactory evidence of an association between work and shoulder, hand and wrist tendinitis, carpal tunnel syndrome and tension neck syndrome. However, they considered that the evidence was tentative and contradictory for lateral epicondylitis and cervical radiculopathy, although plausible biological mechanisms for the development of these disorders were postulated. This contrasts with the findings of the NIOSH (1997) review where considerable evidence for the association between work and lateral epicondylitis was reported.

A Finnish researcher (Viikari-Juntura, 1997) has also summarised a number of existing reviews, supplemented by recent studies that have demonstrated the association found between physical aspects of the work place and the development of musculoskeletal disorders including the neck and upper limbs, as has Buckle (1997) in the U.K.

Data from experimental studies provide supportive evidence and should be used to provide exposure values that are tested in epidemiological studies. It is concluded from the Finnish review of the scientific basis of regulations for the prevention of musculoskeletal disorders (Viikari-Juntura, 1997) that existing scientific knowledge can be used in the development of guidelines that are acceptable and that are considered practical for implementation.

Bovenzi (1998) has reviewed the exposure-response relationship with respect to the hand-arm vibration syndrome. He has concluded that there is epidemiologic evidence for an increased occurrence of peripheral sensorineural disorders in occupational groups working with vibrating tools. An excess risk for wrist osteoarthrosis and for elbow arthrosis and osteophytosis has been reported in workers exposed to shocks and low frequency vibration of high magnitude from percussive tools. Occupational exposure to hand transmitted vibration is significantly associated with an increased occurrence of digital vasospastic disorders, known as vibration-induced white finger.

3.4

INTERVENTIONS IN THE

WORKPLACE

The limited literature on work interventions provides some evidence, both in controlled and uncontrolled studies, of the potential benefits of workplace interventions.

The expert panel concluded that there was good evidence that work system interventions had been shown to be effective for reducing neck and upper limb musculoskeletal disorders, although such interventions were most likely to be successful amongst workers in high risk/ high exposure groups. **It was also considered prudent to reduce problems of discomfort and fatigue through interventions, as this was likely to reduce the subsequent incidence of any upper limb disorders.**

Several field research studies have provided evidence that demonstrates the effects of multi-factorial interventions in the workplace upon exposure to risk factors and reductions in several musculoskeletal health outcomes (National Research Council, 1999). Smith et al. (1999), in the NRC report, provides the evidence showing that some intervention strategies can prevent the development of musculoskeletal disorders in specific industries and occupational groups (e.g. nurses, meatpackers, assembly and postal workers). Examples were found where multiple ergonomics redesign, movement pattern training and physical therapy interventions resulted in a reduction in recorded neck and upper limb musculoskeletal disorders, lost workdays, numbers of days of restricted activity and employee turnover (Harma et al., 1988; Orgel et al., 1992; May and Schwoerer, 1994; Parenmark et al., 1988).

There was also a number of both laboratory and field studies (Smith et al., 1998; Schoenmarklin and Marras, 1989; Keyserling et al., 1993) that identified a reduction in biomechanical stressors following ergonomics redesign (e.g. redesign of hand tools or workstations), thereby reducing the risk of upper limb disorders. For example, Aarås and Oro (1997) compared the muscular load required to operate a traditional computer mouse with a newly developed design. A reduction in the muscular load was observed in the forearms and also in the neck (trapezius). Aarås et al. (1999) then introduced the new mouse design to a group of office workers. The subjects were randomly assigned to an intervention or control group. Six months after the intervention a significant reduction in the intensity and frequency of wrist/hand, forearm, shoulder and neck pain was observed in the group with the new design compared to the control group that used a traditional mouse design.

A recent critical review of the literature on intervention studies was conducted by Norwegian and Swedish researchers (Westgaard and Winkel, 1997). They reviewed studies that had changed job exposures considered harmful to musculoskeletal health. They included interventions on mechanical exposure (e.g. postural load) and other risk factors for musculoskeletal problems; production system and/or organisational culture alterations affecting mechanical exposures; and interventions that attempted to modify the behaviour and/or capacities of individual workers (e.g. exercise/relaxation programmes, physiotherapy or health education). Despite the methodological difficulties in conducting intervention research in the workplace (Rubenowitz, 1997; Zwerling et al., 1997), there was evidence to show that reducing the mechanical exposure(s) resulted in the reduction of neck and upper limb musculoskeletal disorders[4]. These interventions involved either reducing the mechanical exposure directly (through modified workstation design) or indirectly through alterations in organisational culture. Organisational culture was defined by Westgaard and Winkel (1997) as: "Systematic activities of major stakeholders within an organisation, relating to health, safety and environment and comprising measures to influence, e.g. management systems, behaviour and attitudes, for dealing with potential or manifest musculoskeletal health problems of the workforce." Measures included ergonomic programmes with management, ergonomics training and systems for problem identification and solution.

However, it should be noted that the relatively few studies on production system interventions for reducing neck and upper limb musculoskeletal disorders precludes comparison with work organisational culture and mechanical exposure intervention effectiveness (Westgaard and Winkel, 1997).

It was also found that interventions actively including the worker (medical management of workers at risk, physical or active training in worker technique or combinations of these approaches) often achieved a reduction in musculoskeletal problems including those of the neck and upper limbs.

The conclusions from this contemporary and authoritative review were to **focus interventions on factors within the work organisation, not solely on the worker** (e.g. training/work hardening). It was also emphasised that the active support and involvement of the individuals at risk and other stakeholders in the organisations was highly recommended.

Häkkänen et al. (1997), for example, has shown that relatively simple and low-cost ergonomics solutions can result in a reduction in exposure to work risk factors for upper limb musculoskeletal disorders.

---

[4] It was also noted that reductions in mechanical exposure might be most beneficial for musculoskeletal health in work situations where the levels are high.

Examples of the cost effectiveness of ergonomics interventions for these disorders have been reported by, amongst others, Schneider (1998) and Hendrick (1996). The odds of a work related musculoskeletal disorder resulting in lost time without an ergonomics intervention was three times greater than with an intervention (Schneider, 1998). This study also found that the return on investment i.e. the benefit/cost of intervention in an office environment was 17.8 ($1693/$95). Ergonomics intervention to redesign an assembly line process was shown to reduce workers compensation costs for work-related musculoskeletal disorders from $94000 to $12000 in a telecommunications organisation (Hendrick, 1996). Between 1990-1994, ergonomics intervention saved $1.48 million in worker compensation costs for the same organisation.

3.5

SUMMARY - THE WORK-RELATEDNESS OF NECK AND UPPER LIMB DISORDERS

The scientific reports, using defined criteria for causality, established a strong positive relationship between the occurrence of some neck and upper limb musculoskeletal disorders and the performance of work, especially where high levels of exposure to work risk factors were present.

Understanding of the pathogenesis of these disorders varies greatly with regard to the specific condition in question. For many of the disorders, (e.g. carpal tunnel syndrome) the body of knowledge is impressive, bringing together biomechanics, mathematical modelling and direct measurement of physiological and soft tissue changes. These form a coherent argument that is persuasive of the biomechanically induced pathogenesis of such conditions. For those conditions where the knowledge base is smaller, plausible hypotheses do exist and are currently the subject of much research interest.

Both the National Research Council (USA) and the National Institute of Occupational Safety and Health (USA) reports make reference to the potential importance of psychosocial and work organisational factors. Both conclude that there is increasing evidence that these factors are important in the development of work related musculoskeletal disorders. The expert panel has considered these reviews to be helpful in the preparation of this report and agreed with the general findings. The panel further noted the limitations of such reports with respect to the criteria set for inclusion of studies for review.

The expert panel concluded that existing scientific knowledge could be used in the development of preventative strategies. These will be acceptable to many stakeholders and are practical for implementation. There is limited but persuasive evidence on the effectiveness of work system interventions incorporating ergonomics.

RESEARCH

STRATEGIES FOR

PREVENTION

4.1

INTRODUCTION

The strategies have been derived from the following areas:

1. Contemporary Scientific Literature

The evidence relied upon has been identified earlier in this report. Additional sources have been listed below where applicable. The methods used for the literature searches have been included in the appendices.

2. Expert opinion

The nature and extent of the expert views sought has been identified in section 1.

Position papers from established groups have also been considered. For example, the Scientific Committee for Musculoskeletal Disorders of the International Commission on Occupational Health (ICOH) provided a substantive argument regarding both risk factors and prevention (Kilbom et al., 1996). They identified the application of ergonomic principles in the workplace as an important method for prevention.

The International Ergonomics Association[5] has produced relevant review documents and guidance for the assessment of exposure to risk factors for upper limb disorders.

Similarly, employee representative groups (e.g. the European Trade Union Technical Bureau for Health and Safety, TUTB) have provided much supportive material. Examples include Ringelberg and Voskamp (1996) and a series of well informed debates and meetings[6].

3. Existing framework of Member state, European and International Directives, standards and guidance.

A number of European Directives are relevant to prevention (e.g. Manual Handling of Loads, Display Screen Equipment, Use of Work Equipment and Framework Directives) as well as a number of European Standards. Many of these show the direction and support *already* given to workplace surveillance and ergonomic interventions in preventing and controlling musculoskeletal problems.

---

[5] IEA Technical Working Group, Chair: Professor Antonio Grieco, University of Milan, Italy.
[6] See the Newsletter of the European Trade Union Technical Bureau for Health and Safety No. 6,1997 pp2-5; No.4,1996 pp 20-21.

Related guidance and ordinances are available in a number of member states. For example, a recent ordinance from Sweden "Ergonomics for the Prevention of Musculoskeletal Disorders, AFS 1998:1" presents guidance on risk assessment for the postural/biomechanical stressors. It was considered by the panel of expert scientists as an important and well-informed document. Some elements of this ordinance are reflected in this document. Other such guidance includes "Work related upper limb disorders: A guide to prevention" by the HSE in 1990.

4. Existing Practice

Many organisations have sought to implement ergonomic programmes and interventions aimed at primary prevention of the problems. This would suggest that they already believe in the effectiveness of ergonomic and occupational health strategies aimed at preventing the development of this group of disorders. Organisations involved in such programmes provide important role models for others wishing to initiate preventive programmes. That said, it is less clear how beneficial such approaches have been.

The extent and scope of the information and approaches currently advocated has been particularly evident when reviewing "in-house" materials and those freely available from sources such as the internet. Whilst there are few data on the success or usefulness of such materials, they are clearly sought after and widely used. This report might therefore be used to inform, guide and harmonise such

sources. Such a process might be enhanced further through appropriate use of the newly established *Topic Centre on Good Safety Health Practice concerning Musculoskeletal Disorders*. This is a recent initiative from the European Agency for Safety and Health at Work.

5. The needs and capacities of those who may use ergonomics approaches to prevention

Any proposed strategies and guidance designed for the workplace must meet the needs and capacities of those responsible for its application, if it is to be successful. Kilbom (1995) has posed the question thus: "Can the knowledge of the risk factors be operationalised in a way that is sufficiently simple to be useful for persons - labour inspectors, occupational health service staff, safety stewards etc. - with a limited knowledge about musculoskeletal disorders and ergonomics?

Thus this report, unlike most other contemporary reviews, has considered this when proposing possible strategies for prevention.

4.1.1 Practitioners ability to make risk assessment in the workplace:

There is a limited literature on what practitioners can reliably be expected to risk assess in the workplace, particularly with regard to risk factors for musculoskeletal disorders. That said, if action requires risk assessment to be made at the workplace, then an understanding of end-user requirements must be an integral part of the knowledge base required. One recent study from England (Li and Buckle, 1998, 1999) has approached this problem through a participatory approach, whereby a method for the assessment of exposure to risk factors for musculoskeletal problems was developed by practitioners and *for* practitioners. Experts were involved only in facilitation and the subsequent assessment of reliability and validity of the method. Such studies have enabled user requirements to be established.

4.1.2 Methods of Risk Assessment:

Exposures to physical risk factors for work-related musculoskeletal disorders have been assessed with a variety of methods, including pen and paper based observation method, videotaping and computer aided analysis, direct or instrumental techniques, and approaches to self-report assessment. These have been critically reviewed elsewhere (e.g. Li and Buckle, 1999). The application of these techniques in ergonomics and epidemiological studies were considered, and their advantages and shortcomings were highlighted. A strategy that considers both the ergonomics experts' view and the practitioners' needs is therefore required.

According to some research experts, suitable analytical methods are still not available for efficiently reducing and quantifying physical exposure (Radwin et al., 1994). Whilst some observational methods for analysing postures and movements have been developed (e.g. RULA, (McAtamney and Corlett, 1993)) they are often time-consuming and labour intensive (Wiktorin et al., 1995).

Most exposure assessment methods/tools involve two (usually contradictory) qualities, precision and generality (Winkel and Mathiasson, 1994). High generality in an observation method is usually compensated by low sensitivity. For example, OWAS (Karhu et al., 1977) has had a wide range of use but the results can be low in detail. In contrast, NIOSH (Waters et al., 1993) requires detailed information about specific parameters of the posture to give high precision with respect to the defined indices, but no general information about the task.

Burdorf et al. (1992) concluded that some of the 'best known' direct observation methods, such as OWAS and posture targetting, lack precision, are less reproducible in dynamic work situation, are not continuous, and are subject to intra- and inter-observer variability. Hagberg (1988) reviewed published methods for the systematic observation of occupational musculoskeletal loads and found that none of these methods were widely accepted.

More recently, Colombini et al. (1998) prepared a consensus document in association with the International Ergonomics Association technical group for work-related musculoskeletal disorders. It included a review of authoritative checklists and a search for models to describe and evaluate each of the principle risk factors. They defined terms that enable common understanding of the analytical requirements including: *tasks, cycles and technical actions.* They also provided a method for exposure assessment that considers the risk factors of repetitiveness (frequency); force; awkward postures and movements; recovery time in addition to a number of complementary factors (e.g. high precision tasks, vibrations, local compression, blows and wrenching movements).

The authors acknowledged the difficulties involved in validating methods where many interactions occur. They also recognised that, in the absence of a complete epidemiological knowledge base, other areas of knowledge (e.g. fatigue studies) may have to be relied upon in assessing tasks. Nevertheless, this approach is important for setting up exposure assessment methods and demonstrates the need for common definitions and agreed assessment methods for single risk factors. The same research institute (Occhipinti, 1998) has also suggested a formula for an expert risk assessment (OCRA) that considers a number of risk factors (frequency, posture, rest pauses, other factors).

4.1.3 Main criteria for exposure assessment methods:

Some of the major points are summarised below:
- The method has to be cheap, easy to learn and quick to use (Corlett, 1990; Sinclair, 1990, Li and Buckle, 1998)
- The method should be applicable to all sections of working life, and should take environmental and psychosocial aspects into consideration (Rohmert and Landau, 1983)
- The measurements have to be repeatable under described conditions, i.e. within the range of movements normally occurring in the actual work situation (Aarås and Stranden, 1988)
- The recording method should not interfere with the movements being recorded (Aarås and Stranden, 1988) and should not interfere with the worker's work (Wilson, 1990; Kirwan and Ainsworth, 1992)
- The method should have high validity, reliability and sensitivity (Pinzke, 1994)
- Assessment data should be readily coded for storage and analysis (Colombini et al., 1985)

Any action proposed must consider these criteria. The proposals that follow have taken account, wherever possible, of the issues identified above. **It must also be recognised that where there are competing criteria a pragmatic outcome must be sought**. This will, on occasions, necessitate compromises.

4.2

HEALTH AND WORK SYSTEM

ASSESSMENT

This section of the report will address, in particular, issues 1 and 3 of these general requirements.

Generally accepted principles of the management of health and safety at work provide a framework, under which the specific actions required for neck and upper limb disorders may be considered.

The most important aspects of the general requirements can be summarised as follows:

1. Assessment of risk to enable the identification of necessary preventive and protective measures.

2. Make arrangements for putting into practice the health and safety measures identified in (1).

3. Provide appropriate health surveillance of employees where necessary.

4. Provide employees with appropriate information and training about health and safety matters.

5. Review the effects of the changes

4.3

DEFINITION OF RISK AND

CONCEPT OF ACTION ZONES

4.3.1 Risk (and risk factors)

Risk has been defined by Last (1983) as "a probability that an event will occur e.g, that an individual will become ill or die within a stated period of time or age." However, the meaning of risk factor is not as clear, as researchers and authors are not always consistent in their use of the term. In this report it is taken to mean an attribute or an exposure that is not necessarily causal but that does increase the probability of a specific outcome (e.g. the occurrence of a disorder of the upper limb).

4.3.2 Action Zones

Increased exposure to risk factors can be thought of as a basis for establishing priorities for action. Those in the groups with the highest exposure to risk factors would normally be expected to attract the highest priority. Whilst current epidemiological knowledge does not allow a full description of the exposure/dose-response relationship for each risk factor, there was a general recognition amongst the experts that extreme exposure groups both could and should be identified; and that these should be specifically targeted in the first instance([7]).

Targeting those at the extremes of the exposure spectrum has additional advantages as the knowledge, experiences and competence gained will enhance the likelihood of the successful transfer of risk identification and risk removal/reduction strategies to those at lower risk.

Methods and approaches developed elsewhere (including the development of standards) and the experience of the experts has led us to propose a three-zone model for action, for most of the recognised risk factors. The zones may be thought of as:

1	High Risk	This zone identifies those at highest risk for the development of upper limb disorders and where action is almost certainly required.
2	Medium risk	Work factors require close attention and remedial actions may be necessary.
3	Low Risk	Areas of least concern, although some action may be prudent. Assessment may provide useful information to inform workplace interventions elsewhere. Routine assessment and surveillance should be extended to this group.

([7]) The failure to provide full descriptions of exposure/dose-response relationships has generally arisen from the nature of the epidemiological study groups. These have often been selected to compare those at the extremes of the exposure spectrum, and thus give limited understanding of the shape of the exposure-response relationship.

The proposed 3 zone model can be compared with that in the CEN standard: *Safety of Machinery - Ergonomic design principles. Part 1. Terminology and general principles EN 614-1 (1995).*

Red *"The risk of disease or injury is obvious and exposure can not be accepted for any part of the operator population in question"*

Yellow *"There exists a risk of disease or injury that can not be neglected, for the whole or part of the population in question."*

Green *"The risk of disease or injury is negligible or is at an acceptable level for the whole operator population in question."*

It is therefore apparent that similar models are already in use within the framework of European Union action

4.4

ASSESSMENT OF RISK:

WORK SYSTEM ASSESSMENT

In considering the risk assessment of the work system, we have chosen to consider the systematic approach advocated through the discipline of ergonomics. This approach is implicit in many of the existing European Union Health and Safety directives (e.g. Manual Handling of Loads, Display Screen Equipment). It recognises the need to consider the work system as a set of interacting elements, with a strong focus on the needs and capacities of the worker (or equipment user) in both risk assessment and work design.

This approach is endorsed in a number of Council Directives, including 89/391/EEC on the Introduction of measures to encourage improvements in the safety and health of workers at work. Thus Article 6 states:

"(d) adapting the work to the individual, especially as regards the design of work places, the choice of work equipment and the choice of working and production methods, with a view, in particular, to alleviating monotonous work and work at a predetermined work-rate and to reducing their effect on health"

Further, Article 4 of the Manual handling of loads directive states:

"Organization of workstations

Wherever the need for manual handling of loads by workers cannot be avoided, the employer shall organize workstations in such a way as to make such handling as safe and healthy as possible and:

(a) assess, in advance if possible, the health and safety conditions of the type of work involved, and in particular examine the characteristics of loads, taking account of Annex I;

(b) take care to avoid or reduce the risk particularly of back injury to workers, by taking appropriate measures, considering in particular the characteristics of the working environment and the requirements of the activity, ... "

In order to be harmonious new strategies should aim to both support and encourage a similar systematic ergonomics approach.

4.5

DEFINITIONS OF WORK SYSTEM FACTORS TO BE ASSESSED

The interactions between factors in work systems require an understanding of the work organisation, tasks undertaken, workspace and equipment demands as well as their impact on the worker.

Whilst the immediate focus for a risk assessment might be, for example, the posture required to undertake a given task, the wider ergonomic assessment of the work system may enable solutions to be found regarding removal or reduction of risk.

Each physical work factor is thought of as having three dimensions. Thus the posture of the wrist during a task can be thought of as comprising an amplitude/magnitude dimension, a repetition or frequency dimension and a duration dimension. Radwin and Lavender (1999) have developed this concept and the following table 5 is modified from that source and provides some examples of physical exposures.

Whilst this table reflects the dimensions for each physical exposure, others (e.g. Kilbom, 1994) have chosen to express these factors in an alternative form. For example, physical exposure can also be expressed as force x time, posture x time and vibration x time. These generic risk factors can be operationalised in different ways (e.g. average force, repetitions per minute).

4.5.1 Duration of Work

The expert panel discussed the definition of action zones with regard to the duration of working tasks.

PHYSICAL EXPOSURE	PROPERTY		
	Amplitude or Magnitude	Repetition	Duration
Force	Force generated or applied	Frequency of application	Time that force is applied
Posture	Joint angle	Frequency	Time held
Motion	Velocity, acceleration	Frequency of motion	Time of motion exposure
Vibration	Acceleration	Frequency that vibration occurs	Time of vibration exposure

Table 5. The amplitude, frequency and duration of some physical exposures.

It was recognised that there is no standard length of a working shift. Particular difficulties were noted with regard to the application of guidance to part time workers having a number of jobs throughout the day. The expert panel discussed at length the relationship between generic exposure to a task that involves a number of physical exposures (e.g. heavy physical work) versus the duration of exposure to a specific risk factor (e.g. vibration).

It was noted that some epidemiological studies have shown that, when the daily exposure time exceeds 4 hours, the rates of WMSD complaints increase in the shoulder/neck, particularly for seated tasks such as VDU operation (e.g. Winkel and Westgaard, 1992).

The current approach used for setting vibration exposure levels was considered. It was noted that the development of exposure levels and limits for physical agents (e.g. vibration) is based on a similar strategy (see CR 1030-1 and ENV 25349).

Thus although there was some research evidence in support of a duration of exposure(s) of four hours placing work tasks in the high "action" zone, further debate on this issue is required.

Task duration is an important risk factor for disorders of the shoulder/arm, neck, and hand/wrist. This factor should be considered in the exposure assessment of each of these body regions. Since the time available for practitioners to assess a job or task can be very limited, other means of assessing the duration to exposure might have to be sought. These could include worker interviews, organisational records or time sampled observations.

4.5.2 Repetitive work and recovery from work

One of the difficulties in comparing studies is the variation in the interpretation of key concepts. Thus the use of the term repetitive with respect to work has been debated by, amongst others, Mathiassen and Winkel (1991) and Kilbom (1994). The issue of repetitiveness within work is closely linked to the concept of work/recovery. It is, for example, frequently assumed that when a worker is not actively engaged in the task under investigation, then recovery time is being provided. However, this may not be the case if that worker moves from one task to another with similar postural or force demands. **Thus a distinction between repetitive work and work recovery is required when interpreting data and providing recommendations.** Repetitive continuous work was considered, by the expert panel, to be work involving rapid hand movements which were almost continuous and involved rapid steady motion.

Latko et al., (1997) have considered the need for a single metric for assessing exposure to repetitive work. They provide an observational method with decision rules and examples to aid in rating tasks. They also suggest the use of verbal anchors combined with a visual rating scale. They report acceptable levels of sensitivity for the parameters of movement frequency and recovery time in hand intensive tasks. This approach offers much promise in the application of action levels, although research questions still remain regarding the use of such methods by those with little prior experience.

4.5.3 The value of fatigue and fatigue studies

Many of the scientists felt that studies of fatigue were important to assist in setting limits. For example, Westgaard and Winkel (1996) have reviewed existing guidelines for physical exposure, many of which rely on fatigue studies. This was also seen to be coherent with the approach taken in other European Directives and Standard setting groups.

For example, the Council Directive 90/270/EEC on the minimum safety and health requirements for work with display screen equipment includes, in its Annex, a recognition of the importance of fatigue with respect to keyboard use:

"(c) Keyboard. The keyboard shall be tiltable and separate from the screen so as to allow the worker to find a comfortable working position avoiding fatigue in the arms or hands. "

Similarly, the "Safety of machinery - Human physical performance - Part 3

Recommended force limits for machinery operation (prEN 10005-3)" considers one part of the risk assessment (Step C) as follows:

"The risk assessment focuses on musculoskeletal disorders, and is preferentially based on the assumption that decreasing fatigue during work is effective in reducing disorders."

The expert group of scientists felt there was some congruence between epidemiological and experimental data with regard to the relationship between biomechanical and psychophysical factors and the onset of fatigue or disorder. This approach is reflected in the National Research Council report (1999).

Scientists with experience of policy setting affirmed their belief that it was prudent to consider fatigue as a potential precursor to some of the disorders under consideration. This view is also evident in the National Research Council Report (1999).

Where appropriate, therefore, guidance based on fatigue studies or data might be considered.

---

[8] prEN documents are draft standards yet to be agreed by the European Standards Organisations

RESEARCH

5.

RISK FACTORS

REQUIRING ASSESSMENT

5.1

GENERAL ASPECTS OF

POSTURE

5.1.1 Importance of Postural Demands

The importance of postural demands both with regard to the epidemiological/biomechanical literature and any surveillance/risk assessment in the workplace has been considered. **There is an extensive literature on the relationships between adverse postural demands at the workplace and upper limb disorders.**

Key reviews have been identified earlier in this report. The importance of such postural demands is also recognised in documents such as the draft CEN standard "prEN 1005-4 Safety of machinery - Human physical performance Part 4. Evaluation of working postures."

5.1.2 Assessment of Postural Demands

Assessment of posture in epidemiological studies has frequently relied on observational or direct (instrumented) measurement. Any action requires observations to be made in the workplace and appropriate observational methodologies have therefore been considered in this report.

A linear/ordinal scale assessment (developed by the University of Michigan, USA) was considered as an example of a promising methodology (Latko et al., 1997). This approach, developed with the help of experts, might be contrasted with the methods developed by and for practitioners (e.g. Li and Buckle, 1998, 1999).

The Swedish Ordinance (Swedish Ordinance on Ergonomics for the Prevention of Musculoskeletal Disorders AFS 1998:1 Statute Book of the Swedish National Board of Occupational Safety and Health) considered posture definition and the acceptability of postures. For example, prolonged work tasks that required the hand or elbow to be held at or above shoulder height were likely to be considered unacceptable.

5.2

NECK

The uncertainty over the epidemiological data led the expert panel to recommend that a further consideration of the current experimental data should be undertaken. These data might provide additional guidance.

For example, tilting the head/neck forward more than 30° greatly increases the neck extensor fatigue rates, but an angle of around 15° produces almost no subjective discomfort or EMG changes even after 6 hours work (Chaffin, 1973). A recent report indicated that the time spent in forward neck flexion (with the critical angle of 15°) was significantly associated with neck and neck/shoulder disorders (Ohlsson et al., 1995).

The scientists agreed that the epidemiological data were not conclusive with regard to specific neck postures and the risk of developing the disorders under consideration in this report. A summary table (see appendix 4) of postural risk factors for the neck was produced by Hagberg et al. (1995). NIOSH (1997) considered 31 studies of the association between extreme or static posture and neck or neck/shoulder musculoskeletal disorders. Of these, they identified three studies (meeting their criteria for acceptability) that found significant associations between posture variables and neck musculoskeletal disorders. However, none of these studies had reported measures of risk. Despite the limitations of these studies the actions and guidance provided by, for example, the Swedish Ordinance were considered to be appropriate by the expert group.

One further difficulty has been highlighted by Li and Buckle (1998). This relates to the ability of practitioners to make simple and reliable assessments of such postures. They found that it is difficult for the observers to determine a specific neck angle through simple observation, and that practitioners prefer to use descriptive word(s) such as 'excessively bent or twisted' rather than using angular values.

The scientific experts also voiced concern over whether rapid twisting movements at the neck could lead to problems. There appeared to be few data available to assist with risk determination. This is an area that requires further research.

There was a general consensus that work systems requiring restrained postures and limited freedom of movement of the head, neck and shoulders should be an area for risk assessment. Definitions of

high, medium and low risk zones are
thought to require further consideration
for the neck.

5.3

SHOULDERS AND ARMS

Working above shoulder height is widely recognised as a risk factor for shoulder musculoskeletal disorders. A summary table (see appendix 4) of postural risk factors for the shoulder was produced by Hagberg et al. (1995).

NIOSH (1997) concluded that there was evidence for a relationship between repeated or sustained shoulder postures, with greater than 60 degrees of flexion or abduction and shoulder musculoskeletal disorders. They found evidence for both shoulder tendinitis and non-specific shoulder pain. Only one of thirteen studies reviewed failed to show a positive relationship.

The provisional standard prEN 1005-4 (Safety of machinery - Human physical performance Part 4-Evaluation of working postures in relation to machinery) also considers shoulder postures. It suggests that tasks requiring shoulder flexion or abduction of greater than 60 degrees are unacceptable for static posture or high frequency movement (greater than or equal to 2 per minute).

Assessment of postural angles in risk assessment is known to present difficulties for practitioners. Thus, whilst 60 degrees of shoulder flexion or abduction has been cited as a possible border of acceptability, it is unlikely that reliable assessments can be made through observation in the workplace. A better approach is to relate the position of the hands to other body parts. Therefore, the expert panel noted that work at or above shoulder height, for example, could be reliably assessed and might be considered as a posture in the high risk zone.

Reach distance has not been widely recognised as an independent risk factor for shoulder disorders, although a greater reach distance may result in more awkward postures of the back and shoulder. Reach, in combination with load or force exertion, is recognised as a risk factor in directives and guidance that consider manual handling at work.

Highly repetitive arm and shoulder movement increases the risk of shoulder tendon disorders (e.g. Bjelle et al., 1981, Ohlsson et al., 1989, 1994, 1995; NIOSH 1997). However, the movement of the shoulder may be very different (in terms of the pattern and speed) from that of the hand/wrist.

Epidemiological studies have not yet provided sufficient information to define the exposure-response relationship regarding the frequency of repetitive shoulder movements.

The ability of practitioners to reliably assess such patterns suggests that the classification of zones for action should be defined by the pattern or manner of the arm movement, rather than by the number of times the arm moves within a given period (Latko et al., 1997).

NIOSH (1997) reviewed the evidence regarding force/load and duration as risk factors associated with shoulder/arm disorders. They found that there was insufficient evidence to enable firm conclusions to be reached regarding the relationship between force and shoulder disorders. This was because the available studies had a considerable diversity of exposure assessment approaches and health outcomes.

Li and Buckle (1999) have found that practitioners find it difficult to make exposure assessments regarding the force/load and also the duration of the task with respect to the shoulder/arm.

5.4

WRISTS

The expert panel agreed that extremes of wrist movement should be included in risk assessments. This was based on both epidemiological (e.g. NIOSH, 1997) and biomechanical laboratory based data. The NIOSH review concluded that there was an association between any single factor (posture, force or repetition) and hand/wrist tendinitis. They also concluded that there was strong evidence that job tasks requiring a combination of risk factors increase the risk for hand wrist tendinitis. It is important to recognise that whilst the epidemiological evidence is stronger with regard to some disorders (e.g. hand/wrist tendinitis) than to others, there is general agreement that, because of common pathways, **any intervention on this risk factor is likely to have benefits for other upper limb musculoskeletal disorders.**

An earlier review (Hagberg et al., 1995) considered studies that reported postural risk factors for the wrist/hand (see appendix 4).

The expert panel agreed that use of experimental data (e.g. contact pressures and carpal tunnel pressures) should be made for establishing appropriate action levels. It was noted that the levels of carpal tunnel pressure when the wrist is deviated from a neutral position are conservative relative to the mechanical contact pressure at the wrist. It was further recognised that the biomechanical and epidemiological data are consistent with regard to hand/wrist tendinitis.

Difficulties exist with respect to the assessment of wrist movements and postures. Direct measurement is both difficult and costly (Li and Buckle, 1999).

Thus whilst the epidemiological and biological evidence in support of the need for action is strong, there are difficulties in providing suitable tools to allow risk assessment to be made in the work place. Laboratory and epidemiological research studies may have access to sophisticated methods for wrist movement, but the practitioner is the workplace is often limited to direct observational techniques.

Li and Buckle (1999) have shown that practitioners have great difficulty in assessing some aspects of wrist posture. This is important because some methods propose the use of precise set boundaries between a 'good' and 'bad' wrist posture (e.g. RULA (McAtamney and Corlett, 1993.)) The epidemiological basis for this is unclear, but it is evident (Li and Buckle,

1999) that it is difficult for an observer to 'measure', through observation, whether the wrist is within, or beyond, 15° or 20° from its neutral position, during work.

An alternative approach, that has been found acceptable to practitioners, has been to assess wrist posture using descriptive terms. The descriptors used are derived from studies that have used 'think aloud' protocols (Li and Buckle, 1998).

Repetition has been widely recognised as a risk factor associated with both hand/wrist tendinitis and carpal tunnel syndrome, especially when in combination with other task factors such as force and posture.

In some studies (e.g. Silverstein et al., 1986) high-repetitive tasks have been defined as those with a work cycle time of less than 30 seconds or with more than 50% of the cycle time involved in performing the same motion pattern. However, in many work situations, a work cycle may not exist, or if it does, work cycle time may vary periodically. This makes it difficult to assess within a limited observation period.

Recent research (Latko et al., 1997) has used verbal descriptors in conjunction with visual analogue scales to enable exposure assessments to be made. Extreme exposures for hand/wrist repetitive movement have therefore been defined using such descriptors (i.e. Work involving rapid and steady hand movements that are almost continuous). Such exposures may place the worker in the high risk zone.

Some authors have also identified the importance of high wrist velocities and accelerations (e.g. Marras and Schoenmarklin, 1993; Malchaire and Cock, 1996). Further research on these factors is required to enable guidance to be developed.

The importance of force as a risk factor associated with hand/wrist musculoskeletal disorders has been recognised by NIOSH (1997). The consistency of the relationship is reflected in the criteria used to assess the strength of the evidence (described earlier in this report). Nevertheless the exposure response relationship is complex as other risk factors are likely to be present in any study group.

These problems are also recognised in a draft CEN standard "Safety of machinery - Human physical performance - Part 3 Recommended force limits for machinery operation (prEN 10005-3)". Whilst force limits have been proposed they require careful use of factors such as the velocity, the frequency and the duration of action. Further modifications are suggested for the tolerability of body tissues as well as a safety margin addressing acceptability. It has also been recognised that the guidance given in this draft standard assumes that an optimal posture can be achieved for the force exertion.

The scientists agreed that there was a need to combine and then synthesise both epidemiological and experimental data in this area.

The assessment of force at the hand is accepted as being methodologically difficult. It should be recognised that the actual load or mass handled can be different from the force exerted by hand. For example, the mass of a power tool may be 3 kg, but the effective load at the wrist/hand will also depend on the centre of gravity with respect to the hand when the tool is in use. Similarly, the force on the hand is also influenced by the force exerted on the tool when in use. Thus the force, which is a risk factor for the hand/wrist, cannot necessarily be recorded directly from the weight/mass of the external load.

It has therefore proved scientifically difficult to evaluate the forces required to carry out tasks at the workplace. Thus, surrogates for these values have frequently been sought (e.g. the perceived effort reported by the worker or estimates provided by observers).

For action to be effective it was considered unfeasible, in most instances, to expect assessors in the workplace to measure the actual forces required. Therefore, guidance would be needed on how to obtain suitable force estimates based on worker perceptions or observer estimates. Similarly, it was recognised by the expert panel that guidance might be required for upper and lower limits of force applications on typical jobs. These may have to be industry or sector specific.

The Swedish ordinance (Ergonomics for the Prevention of Musculoskeletal Disorders, AFS 1998:1), which has a three-zoned system, was considered as a possible model, although some additional parameters (e.g. mechanical pressure on the wrist) might be used to further this model.

Some epidemiological reports have suggested that, for the hand/wrist exposure, high-force jobs are those with estimated average hand force requirements of more than 4 kilogrammes of force (kgf) and low-force jobs are those with hand force requirements below 1 kgf (Silverstein et al., 1986). Chiang et al. (1993) used a lower force cut off (3kgf) for defining their high force exposure groups and showed significant associations with hand/wrist musculoskeletal disorders. Silverstein et al. (1986) reported substantially greater odds ratios than did Chiang et al. (1993) with respect to force.

The TUTB (Ringelberg and Voskamp, 1996) advanced a set of proposals for integrating ergonomic principles into C standards for machinery design. They suggested that operators who have to lift items of more than 3 kg and/or operators having to exert a hand-arm force of more than 20 Newtons should have a risk evaluation (see also prEN 1005-2)

It is considered that the setting of a 4 kgf high risk action zone would be appropriate to ensure that those at greater risk were identified, although a lower force (as suggested by Chiang et al. 1993) might be considered prudent.

5.5

INTERACTIONS

The need to consider the interactions between potential risk factors was referred to frequently throughout the discussions with the expert panel. For example, whilst force and posture are likely to be assessed separately in the workplace, their interactions are undoubtedly of importance (Haselgrave, 1992; Silverstein et al., 1986) Nevertheless, their separate assessment in the workplace may well provide important pointers for potential areas of intervention.

5.6

HAND ARM VIBRATION

(HAND-TRANSMITTED

VIBRATION)

Table 6. The Stockholm Workshop scale for staging cold-induced Raynaud's phenomenon in the hand-arm vibration syndrome. In CEN CR12349:1996 E.

Stage	Grade	Symptoms
0	-	No attacks
1	Mild	Occasional attacks affecting only the tips of one or more fingers
2	Moderate	Occasional attacks affecting distal and middle (rarely also proximal) phalanges of one or more fingers
3	Severe	Frequent attacks affecting all phalanges of most fingers
4	Very severe	As in stage 3, with trophic skin changes in the fingertips

Assessment of Vibration at the Hand

The CEN report entitled "Mechanical vibration - Guide to the health effects of vibration on the human body" (see CR 12349, 1996) found that powered processes and tools that expose the operator to hand/arm vibration were widespread. Exposure can arise from rotating and percussive tools as well as vibrating work pieces and controls. It is estimated that 1.7 % to 3.6% of the work force in Europe and in the USA are exposed to potentially harmful hand transmitted vibration.

The knowledge base relating to the exposure to vibration at the hand interface and its effects on biological tissues is well established and it is generally recognised that **excessive exposure may result in disturbances to finger blood circula-**tion and also in neurological and locomotor functions of the hand and arm **(Bovenzi, 1998).** The potential disorders resulting from exposure to vibration, therefore, are not only musculoskeletal in nature.

It was noted that whilst the draft ISO standard for Vibration should pertain to all biological effects of exposure, in reality the data are only satisfactory for vascular disorders. For vascular disorders well-defined acute and long-term outcomes are apparent (see table 6) and both epidemiological and laboratory data are coherent with regard to this.

Dose-response relationships have been established which are now embodied in the draft ISO/CEN Standards. The exposure to vibration is further to be considered under the draft proposal from the European Union on Physical agents

(Council of the European Union, 94/C 230/03, 1994).

The relationship between vibration and other physical risk factors was considered. **For carpal tunnel syndrome the combination of vibration with some other physical factors may lead to a doubling of the risk.** The CEN (CR 12349:1996 E) suggests that physical stressors acting on the hand and wrist (repetitive movements, forceful gripping, awkward postures), in combination with vibration may cause carpal tunnel syndrome in workers handling vibrating tools.

Guidance is needed for practitioners on the vibration characteristics of tools.

Databases are currently being established that will make available both manufacturer data and field data (e.g. Sweden, http://umetech.niwl.se/Vibration/HAVHome.html). Thus, the daily energy-equivalent total vibration values will be provided for practitioners.

It was further recognised that the method of use of a tool, the piece that the tool was working on and issues of maintenance may all significantly affect the extent of risk associated with those tasks.

Methods for assessing human exposure to mechanical vibration and shock are contained in ISO/CD 5349-2 (1999). This provides appropriate advice regarding the use of accelerometers to assess vibration characteristics at the "hand", methods of mounting the accelerometers on the vibrating equipment or surface, problems of processing the data and evaluation of uncertainties. It also details the calculation of daily vibration exposure (8 hour energy equivalent acceleration of vibration) and estimated daily vibration exposure with respect to risk of finger blanching (based on ISO/CD 5349-1).

Assessment of the workers exposure to hand/arm vibration requires considerable practitioner expertise and access to technical equipment. It is difficult or impossible to gain any meaningful 'measure' of the exposure to vibration or the characteristics of the vibration through observational methods. Therefore, in the absence of appropriate direct measurement devices (accelerometers) and technical knowledge, subjective judgements may be needed.

The need to include vibration as a risk factor for upper limb musculoskeletal disorders, to assess exposure and take appropriate action is convincing based on the evidence. However, difficulties exist with the application of risk assessment amongst practitioner groups without access to appropriate equipment.

5.7

WORK ORGANISATION AND

PSYCHOSOCIAL FACTORS

Whilst other areas of action have been considered with reference to body location, the final section is of a generic nature and has been considered separately. Both work organisation and psychosocial work factors are recognised as associated with these disorders (Devereux and Buckle, 1998; Smith and Carayon, 1996). However, the lack of standardisation of both concepts and terminology has generated difficulties when seeking to interpret research findings and to generate action limits. Hagberg et al. (1995) have discussed the meaning of work organisational and psychosocial work: "*Psychosocial factors at work are the subjective aspects as perceived by workers and the managers. They often have the same names as the work organisation factors, but are different in that they carry 'emotional' value for the worker. Thus, the nature of the supervision can have positive or nega-*

tive psychosocial effects (emotional stress), while the work organisation aspects are just descriptive of how the supervision is accomplished and do no not carry emotional value. Psychosocial factors are the individual subjective perceptions of the work organisation factors."

It must be noted that this is not a globally accepted definition but is considered to be suitable for the purposes of this report.

Theorell (1996) considered the possible mechanisms behind the relationship between the demand-control-support psychosocial model of Karasek (1979) and Karasek and Theorell (1990) and disorders of the musculoskeletal system. In this model, both quantitative and qualitative psychological demands have greater adverse consequences if they occur jointly with low decision latitude (i.e. little opportunity to influence decisions in the job). He identified three different kinds of mechanisms that might relate psychosocial factors to musculoskeletal disorder symptoms. The three mechanisms postulated are physiological, leading to organic changes; physiological mechanisms that influence pain perception; and sociopsychological conditions that are of significance to the individual's possibility of coping with the illness. The latter are of particular importance in rehabilitation. He also identified a further complication to understanding in that the mechanisms generating acute conditions are often different to those perpetuating pain and creating chronic conditions. It would appear that more physiological studies are needed in the exploration of possible pathways.

The International Labour Office (ILO) 1998 publication "Work Organization and Ergonomics" emphasised the potential importance of integrating ergonomics and work organisation to achieve better physical conditions, better social relationships and equipment and better work organisation practices (Buchanan et al., 1998). The approach advocated requires further debate, particularly with regard to its role in preventive strategies.

As noted earlier (see section on work relatedness and epidemiology) there is limited research on the relationship between work organisation and neck and upper limb musculoskeletal disorders although there is plausibility in such a relationship. For example, the effect of an organisation downsizing has been shown, in a follow-up study in Finland, to increase the risk substantially for sick leave due to musculoskeletal disorders. The disorders in this study were classified under the International Classification of Diseases (1977 revision) (Vahtera et al., 1997).

It has been postulated that work organisational factors may affect short and long term reactions to mental stress[9]. These may subsequently affect the development of upper limb disorders. In addition, work organisation factors may directly influence physical work risk factors for neck and upper limb disorders such as posture and duration of repetitive movements (Bongers et al., 1993; Smith and Carayon, 1996).

A report aimed at investigating time constraints and autonomy at work in the European Union has shown that time constraints are clearly rising (Dhondt, 1998). Less firm judgements can be made regarding job autonomy due to differences in definitions and instruments used in surveys. It is concluded that high strain working conditions are increasing in the European Union but that further research is required to clarify the observed trends.

An EU community action (Council directive 93/104/EC on Working Time) draws attention to alleviating monotonous work and work at predetermined work-rates, and thus has a direct bearing on exposure to the risk factors described in this report.

An ergonomics approach to work (re)design on organisational factors has been shown to be effective when there is a high commitment from stakeholders, and when multiple strategies are used to reduce identified risk factors (Westgaard and Winkel, 1997). This strategy is echoed by the International Labour Organisation (1998) who states that "problems are interrelated – solutions are multiple". Participatory ergonomics offers the potential for developing such an integrated approach (for a review, see Haines and Wilson, 1998). It is recommended that future interventions consider the benefits of such a strategy.

A recent report (Parkes et al., 1998) by the U.K. Health and Safety Executive includes industrial case studies. These have

---

[9] Mental stress has been defined under ISO 10075:1991(E) as "The total of all assessable influences impinging upon a human being from external sources and affecting it mentally".

demonstrated the value of work redesign by organisational interventions. This enabled improved management of risk for psychosocial work factors.

The NIOSH (1997) and National Research Council (1999) reviews on work-related musculoskeletal disorders provide supporting evidence for a relationship between psychosocial work factors and neck and upper limb musculoskeletal disorders. There is, however, a re-iteration of the need for agreed definitions with respect to psychosocial factors.

Subjective, perceived workload is associated with a variety of disorders. However, mental workload cannot easily be measured and workload can mean different things to different people. That is, workload is not merely a property of the task, but of the task, the human and their interaction (Tulga and Sheridan, 1980). Although no single psychosocial or work organisational factor is the predominant cause of disorders (Hales et al., 1994), based on the current knowledge, some psychosocial work factors should still be assessed.

Their importance in the current European Directives has already been identified. For example:

"Manual Handling of Loads

1. Requirements of the activity

The activity may present a risk particularly of back injury if it entails one or more of the following requirements: - over-frequent or over-prolonged physical effort involving in particular the spine, - an insufficient bodily rest or recovery period, -

excessive lifting, lowering or carrying distances, - a rate of work imposed by a process which cannot be altered by the worker."

Existing Council Directive 93/104/EC (23 November 1993) concerning certain aspects of the organisation of working time, has also identified psychological aspects of work as issues to be addressed:

"Article13

Pattern of work

Member States shall take the measures necessary to ensure that an employer who intends to organize work according to a certain pattern takes account of the general principle of adapting work to the worker, with a view, in particular, to alleviating monotonous work and work at a predetermined work-rate, depending on the type of activity, and of safety and health requirements, especially as regards breaks during working time."

Bongers et al. (1993) and Lindström (1994) have provided criteria for good work organisation and psychosocial factors. These may form the basis for further consultation on these issues.

In this report, it is suggested that any guidance should be limited to the factors of job decision latitude, job demands and social support. A similar approach has been taken in the Swedish Ordinance on Ergonomics for the Prevention of Musculoskeletal Disorders AFS 1998:1 (Statute Book of the Swedish National Board of Occupational Safety and Health).

It is recognised that assessment of psychosocial work factors is subjective and contextual. However, these factors have been associated with the disorders under review here and, thus, should be addressed. It is suggested that further consultations are held on this topic.

RESEARCH

surveillance appropriate to the health and safety risks they incur at work, measures shall be introduced in accordance with national law and/or practices.

2. The measures referred to in paragraph 1 shall be such that each worker, if he so wishes, may receive health surveillance at regular intervals.

3. Health surveillance may be provided as part of a national health system. "

The major goals of any surveillance system (Hagberg et al., 1995) are to achieve early identification of work related musculoskeletal disorders and symptoms as well as their risk factors. Additional goals include:

- Determination of the size of the problem
- Identifying those at most risk
- Identifying those at least risk (to help inform the change process)
- Systematic description of the risk factors to inform change and prioritise needs
- Assessment of change over time and success of preventative changes and actions

6.

HEALTH AND RISK

SURVEILLANCE

The importance of health and risk surveillance is both recognised and established in some existing directives. For example, Council Directive 89/391/EEC on the introduction of measures to encourage improvements in the safety and health of workers at work has:

"Article 14
Health surveillance

1. To ensure that workers receive health

Surveillance data collection methods must be practical, uniform and be able to be used rapidly, even if this has some effect on their accuracy (see also Last, 1983). Surveillance methods are characterised as either passive or active. Passive methods usually rely on existing data sources (e.g. occupational health records, sickness absence records, routine risk assessments). Active methods may also include specifically designed methods and tools with information being collected from, for example, particular sections of a workforce.

One example of this approach already in action comes from the European Committee for Standardization (CEN). They have identified the need for health surveillance with regard to hand arm vibration exposure and the associated injuries or disorders (see CEN CR 12349, 1996). A handbook on surveillance for work-related musculoskeletal disorders is currently being developed by the International Commision on Occupational Health (ICOH) and the International Ergonomics Association (IEA.)

It should be noted, however, that whilst the potential benefits of health and risk surveillance programmes for these disorders are considerable, the actual benefits are largely unknown. An evaluation programme is therefore warranted.

It is suggested that any preventive strategy relating to neck and upper limb musculoskeletal disorders makes full reference to an appropriate approach to surveillance.

The process of consultation has enabled views to be gathered from a wide range of experts and organisations. The feedback has been highly supportive of the methods and findings of this report. However, there is a growing belief that the social dimension to these problems may require additional strategies for prevention. In particular the recognition that, with respect to public health, general social factors (e.g. poor economic circumstances, low levels of education, poor connections with the labour market) contribute to ill-health by increasing the vulnerability of large populations. This happens independently of the working conditions and will limit the potential effectiveness of interventions directed specifically at the work place.

Similarly, within organisations the ability to recognise, adopt and implement the available ergonomics advice also requires further consideration. For example, the balance between analysis and action when limited resources are available or the potential for incorporating approaches into existing management and organisational thinking have not been discussed within this report, yet they remain vital components if prevention strategies are to be optimised.

RESEARCH

7.

DEVELOPMENTS IN THE

CONTEXT OF OTHER

EUROPEAN UNION

INITIATIVES

Finally, the complex nature of existing directives, member state regulations and guidance and current standards has highlighted the need for further harmonisation. Whilst these have been recognised, it is considered outside of the scope of this report to resolve these issues.

RESEARCH

8.

Consistently reported risk factors requiring consideration in the work system are postural (notably relating to the shoulder and wrist), force applications at the hand, hand arm exposure to vibration, direct mechanical pressure on tissues, effects of a cold work environment and work organisational and psychosocial issues. The limited understanding of interactions between these variables mean that exposure-response relationships are difficult to deduce. However, those workers at high risk can be identified using the current knowledge base.

Scientists with experience of policy setting affirmed their belief that it was prudent to consider fatigue as a potential precursor to some of the disorders. Its use in surveillance programmes was also suggested. The role of fatigue is evident in some existing European health and safety directives and standards.

SUMMARY - STRATEGIES FOR PREVENTION

This section has focussed on the assessment of risk factors, preventive and protective measures and the provision of appropriate surveillance. It recognises the need to provide appropriate information and training.

The report has considered the ability of those at the workplace (e.g. practitioners, worker representatives) to make risk assessments. Advice has been provided as to how such assessments could be made.

General Issues of Exposure: Although there was some research evidence in support of a duration of exposure(s) of four hours placing work tasks in the high "action" zone, further debate on this issue is required. A distinction between repetitive work and work recovery is required when interpreting data and in providing recommendations.

Neck: The expert panel agreed that the epidemiological data were not conclusive with regard to specific neck postures and the risk of developing the disorders under consideration in this report. The uncertainty over the epidemiological data led the group to recommend that a further consideration of the current experimental data should be undertaken.

Shoulders: Working above shoulder height is widely recognised as a risk factor for shoulder musculoskeletal disorders. Recommendations for action on posture have been made. Epidemiological studies have not yet provided sufficient information to define the exposure-response relationship regarding the frequency of repetitive shoulder movements or for force exertions at the shoulder.

Wrists: The expert panel agreed that extremes of wrist movement should be included in risk assessments and that any intervention on this risk factor is likely to have benefits for other upper limb musculoskeletal disorders. Biomechanical and epidemiological data support each other with regard to hand/wrist tendinitis. However, whilst the epidemiological and biological evidence in support of the need for action is strong, there are difficulties in providing suitable tools to allow risk assessment to be made in the work place. The importance of force as a risk factor for hand/wrist musculoskeletal disorders was recognised and the setting of a high-risk action zone for force at the wrist was seen as feasible.

Hand Arm Vibration: The knowledge base relating to the exposure to vibration at the hand interface and its effects on biological tissues is substantial. Excessive exposure may result in disturbances to finger blood circulation and also in neurological and locomotor functions of the hand and arm. Guidance is needed for practitioners on the vibration characteristics of tools. The

inclusion of vibration as a risk factor for upper limb musculoskeletal disorders and the need to assess exposure and seek appropriate action is convincing, based on the current evidence. Some difficulties exist with the availability of specialist equipment required for risk assessment, although newly developed databases provide a good source of information for the vibration characteristics of powered tools.

Organisational and Psychosocial work factors: Assessment of psychosocial work factors is subjective and contextual. However, these factors are associated with the disorders and should be addressed. The importance of work organisational factors is evident in a number of EU Directives and their relationship with these disorders has been demonstrated in a number of epidemiological studies. Plausible hypotheses and mechanisms exist to explain these relationships but further research and wider consultation on preventive strategies are required.

Interventions: The report has found good evidence in support of an ergonomics work system approach. This is harmonious with a number of European Union directives and standards. Such an approach must take due regard of the work system risk factors identified in this report. Participatory ergonomics offers the potential for developing an integrated approach.

Appropriate ergonomics intervention on the work system risk factors for any single specific disorder is also likely to confer benefits with regard to other disorders. For example, reducing the exposure to hand arm vibration will not only reduce the likelihood of the development of Raynaud's disease, but also may also reduce the need for high force exertion at the hand and, thus, reduce the risk for hand/wrist tendinitis. Such benefits arise because of the common pathways leading to some of the disorders.

The importance of a health and risk surveillance programme has been emphasised, and is supported by both existing European Union directives and a number of internationally recognised professional commissions and associations. The provision of methods to enable organisations to undertake such surveillance is considered to be an additional and important factor in determining both the nature and scope of any preventive strategies.

Many organisations have sought to implement ergonomic programmes and interventions aimed at primary prevention of the problems. This would suggest that they already believe in the effectiveness of ergonomic and occupational health strategies aimed at preventing the development of this group of disorders. Organisations involved in such programmes provide important role models for others wishing

to initiate preventive programmes. It is less clear how beneficial such approaches have been although there are a number of studies that demonstrate the cost-effectiveness of an ergonomics approach. Within organisations the ability to recognise, adopt and implement the available ergonomics advice also requires further consideration.

The process of dissemination might be enhanced through appropriate use of the newly established *Topic Centre on Good Safety and Health Practice concerning Musculoskeletal Disorders*. This is a recent initiative from the European Agency for Safety and Health at Work.

There is a growing belief that the social dimension to these problems may require additional strategies for prevention. In particular, the recognition that general social factors (e.g. poor economic circumstances, low levels of education, poor connections with the labour market) contribute to ill-health by increasing the vulnerability of large populations. This happens independently of the working conditions and may limit the potential effectiveness of interventions directed specifically at the work place.

RESEARCH

9.

CONCLUSIONS

9.1

DIAGNOSTIC CRITERIA

There is little evidence of the use of standardised criteria across member states. This is reflected in the nationally reported data as well as the research literature and makes comparison between member states difficult. Current studies that have reached consensus diagnostic criteria should be disseminated widely for further consultation, with a view to standardisation. This report recognises that the criteria for primary preventative use in workplace surveillance and occupational health will be different from the criteria used for some clinical interventions.

9.2

SIZE OF THE PROBLEM

the same methodological criteria have reported large differences in prevalence rates between member states. The reasons for this require further investigation.

A number of epidemiological studies have found that women are at higher risk for work related neck and upper limb disorders, although associations with workplace risk factors are generally found to be stronger than gender factors. The importance of gender differences, and their implication for work system design, is largely outside the scope of this report but requires more substantial debate.

There is substantial evidence within the EU member states that neck and upper limb musculoskeletal disorders are a significant problem with respect to ill health and associated costs within the workplace. It is likely that the size of the problem will increase as exposure to work-related risk factors for these conditions is increasing within the European Union.

Estimates of the cost of these problems are limited. Where data do exist (e.g. the Nordic countries and the Netherlands) the cost has been estimated at between 0.5% and 2% of GNP.

The lack of standardised diagnostic criteria makes comparison of data between member states difficult and little is known of the validity of the reported data. This also makes it difficult to assess the extent of ill health and associated costs within the workplace. Those studies that have used

9.3

PATHOGENESIS

Understanding of the pathogenesis of these disorders varies greatly with regard to the specific condition in question. For many of the disorders, (e.g. carpal tunnel syndrome) the body of knowledge is impressive, bringing together biomechanics, mathematical modelling and direct measurement of physiological and soft tissue changes. These form a coherent argument that is persuasive of the biomechanically induced pathogenesis of such conditions. For those conditions where the knowledge base is smaller, plausible hypotheses do exist and are currently the subject of much research interest.

9.4

WORK-RELATEDNESS

sure-response relationships are difficult to deduce. However, those workers at high risk can be identified using the current knowledge base.

The scientific reports, using defined criteria for causality, established a strong positive relationship between the occurrence of some neck and upper limb musculoskeletal disorders and the performance of work, especially where high levels of exposure to work risk factors were present. Thus the identification of workers in the extreme exposure categories should become a priority for any preventative strategy.

Consistently reported risk factors requiring consideration in the work system are postural (notably relating to the shoulder and wrist), force applications at the hand, hand arm exposure to vibration, direct mechanical pressure on tissues, effects of a cold work environment and work organisational and psychosocial issues. The limited understanding of interactions between these variables means that expo-

9.5

SCOPE FOR PREVENTION

The expert panel concluded that existing scientific knowledge could be used in the development of preventative strategies. These will be acceptable to many stakeholders and are practical for implementation. There is limited but persuasive evidence on the effectiveness of work system interventions incorporating ergonomics. The ergonomics work system approach must take due regard of the work system risk factors identified in this report and a three level model of risk assessment has been proposed.

Appropriate ergonomics intervention on the work system risk factors for any single specific disorder is also likely to confer benefits with regard to other disorders. For example, reducing the exposure to hand arm vibration will not only reduce the likelihood of the development of Raynaud's disease, but also may also reduce the need for high force exertion at the hand and, thus, reduce the risk for hand/wrist tendinitis. Such benefits arise because of the common pathways leading to some of the disorders.

Scientists with experience of policy setting affirmed their belief that it was prudent to consider fatigue as a potential precursor to some of the disorders. Its use in surveillance programmes was also suggested. The role of fatigue is evident in some existing European health and safety directives and standards.

Many organisations have sought to implement ergonomic programmes and interventions aimed at primary prevention of the problems. This would suggest that they already believe in the effectiveness of ergonomic and occupational health strategies aimed at preventing the development of this group of disorders. Organisations involved in such programmes provide important role models for others wishing to initiate preventive programmes. That said, it is less clear how beneficial such approaches have been. Within organisations the ability to recognise, adopt and implement the available ergonomics advice also requires further consideration.

The importance of a health and risk surveillance programme has been emphasised, and is supported by both existing European Union directives and a number of internationally recognised professional commissions and associations.

The report has considered the ability of those at the workplace (e.g. practitioners, worker representatives) to make risk assessments. Advice as to how such assessments could be made, given these restrictions, has been provided. The agreement of valid, standardised methods for the evaluation of working conditions and assessment of risk factors is required.

The report has not identified a specific form of action. However, the report has provided a basis on which action could be formulated and existing European directives on health and safety issues are consistent with the recommendations made. Those organisations that have implemented ergonomic programmes for prevention should be encouraged to help promote any future action.

The process of dissemination might be enhanced through appropriate use of the newly established *Topic Centre on Good Safety and Health Practice concerning Musculoskeletal Disorders*. This is a recent initiative from the European Agency for Safety and Health at Work.

Finally, there is a growing belief that the social dimension to these problems may require additional strategies for prevention. In particular, the recognition that general social factors (e.g. poor economic circumstances, low levels of education, poor connections with the labour market) contribute to ill-health by increasing the vulnerability of large populations. This happens independently of the working conditions.

Human-Computer Interaction 1999; 11: 79-94.

Aarås A, Stranden E. Measurement of postural angles during work. Ergonomics 1988; 31: 935-944.

Aarås A, Westgaard RH. Further studies of postural load and musculoskeletal injuries of workers at an electro-mechanical assembly plant. Applied Ergonomics 1987; 18: 211-219.

Aarås A, Westgaard RH, Stranden E. Work load on local body structures assessed by postural angles measurements. In: Corlett EN, Wilson J, Manenica I, eds. New methods in applied ergonomics, Philadelphia: Taylor & Francis, 1987: 273-278.

Aarås A, Westgaard RH, Stranden E. Postural angles as an indication of postural load and muscular injury in occupational work situations. Ergonomics 1000, 01: 915-933.

Armstrong TJ, Chaffin DB. An investigation of the relationship between displacements of the finger and wrist joints and the extrinsic finger flexor tendons. Journal of Biomechanics 1978; 11: 119-128.

Armstrong TJ, Chaffin DB. Some biomechanical aspects of the carpal tunnel. Journal of Biomechanics 1979; 12: 567-570.

Armstrong T, Castelli W, Evans G, Dias-Perez R. Some histological changes in carpal tunnel contents and their biomechanical implications. Journal of Occupational Medicine 1984; 26: 197-201.

10.

REFERENCES

Aarås A, Ro O. Workload when using a mouse as an input device. International Journal of Human-Computer Interaction 1997; 9: 105-118.

Aarås A, Ro O, Thoresen M. Can a more neutral position of the forearm when operating a computer mouse reduce the pain level for visual display unit operators? A prospective epidemiological intervention study. International Journal of

Armstrong TJ, Buckle P, Fine LJ, Hagberg M, Jonsson B, Kilbom Å, Kuorinka I, Silverstein BA, Sjøgaard G, Viikari-Juntura E.. A conceptual model for work-related neck and upper-limb musculoskeletal disorders. Scandinavian Journal of Work Environment and Health 1993; 19: 73-84.

Ashton-Miller JA. Response of muscle and tendon to injury and overuse. Work-related musculoskeletal disorders: report, workshop summary, and workshop papers. National Research Council, Washington D.C: National Academy Press, 1999; 73-97.

Backman C, Boquist L, Friden J, Lorentzon R, Toolanen G. Chronic achilles paratendonitis with tendinosis: an experimental model in the rabbit. Journal of Orthopedics Research 1998; 8: 541-754.

Bateman E. Neurological painful conditions affecting the shoulder. Clin Orthop Relat Res 1983; 173: 44-54.

Bergenheim M, Johansson H, Pedersen J. The role of the g-system for improving information transmission in populations of la afferents. Neuroscience Research; 23: 207-215.

Besson JM. The Neurobiology of pain. The Lancet 1999; 353: 1610-1615.

Beyer JA, Wright IS. The hyperabduction syndrome: with special feature to its relationship to Raynaud's syndrome. Circulation: The Journal of the American Heart Association 1951; 4: 161-172.

Bishu RR, Manjunath SG, Hallbeck MS. A fatigue mechanics approach to cumulative trauma disorders. In: Das B, ed. Advances in industrial ergonomics, New York: Taylor & Francis, 1990: 215-222.

Bjelle A, Hagberg M, Michaelsson G. Occupational and individual factors in acute shoulder-neck disorders among industrial workers. British Journal of Industrial Medicine 1981; 38: 356-363.

Blair S. Pathophysiology of cumulative trauma disorders: Some possible humoral and nervous system mechanisms. In: Moon SD, Sauter SL, eds. Beyond biomechanics: Psychosocial aspects of musculoskeletal disorders in office work. London: Taylor & Francis, 1996: 91-97.

Blatter BM, Bongers PM. Work related neck and upper limb symptoms(RSI): high risk occupations and risk factors in the Dutch working population. TNO Arbeid rapport projectnr. 4070117, Hoofddorp, The Netherlands, 1999.

Blatter BM, Bongers PM, de Witte H. Work related neck and upper limb symptoms (RSI): high risk occupations and risk factors in the Belgian working population. TNO Arbeid rapport projectnr. 4070117\r9900409, Hoofddorp, The Netherlands, 1999.

Bongers PM, de Winter CR, Kompier MAJ, Hildebrandt VH. Psychosocial factors at work and musculoskeletal disease. Scandinavian Journal of Work Environment and Health 1993; 19: 297-312.

Borg R, Burr H. Danske lønmodtageres arbejdsmiljø og helbred 1990-1995 (Danish Employees Working Environment and Health Study 1990-1995). National

Institute of Occupational Health, Denmark, 1997.

Borghouts JAJ, Koes BW, Vondeling H, Bouter LM. Cost of illness of neck pain in the Netherlands in 1996. Pain 1999; 80: 629-636.

Bovenzi M. Exposure-response relationship in the hand-arm vibration syndrome: an overview of current epidemiological research. International Archives of Occupational and Environmental Health 1998; 71: 509-519.

Bovenzi M, Lindsell C, Griffin M. Duration of acute exposures to vibration and finger circulation Scandinavian Journal of Work Environment and Health 1998; 24:130-137.

Bovenzi, M. Italian statistics for compensated occupational diseases. Personal Communication, 1999.

Brammer AJ, Taylor W, Lundborg G. Sensorineural stages of the hand-arm vibration syndrome. Scandinavian Journal of Work Environment and Health 1987; 13: 279-283.

Broberg, E. Anmälda arbetssjukdomar i Norden 1990-1992 (Reported occupational diseases in the Nordic countries 1990-1992 - with english summaries and legends). The Nordic Council of Ministers, (TemaNord 1996:545), 1996.

Broberg, E. Arbetssjukdomar och arbetsolyckor 1995 (Occupational diseases and occupational accidents 1995). Official Statistics of Sweden, National Board of Occupational Safety and Health. Sweden: Statistics Sweden, 1997.

Buchanan D, Cressey P, Hiba JC, Scmid F, Wilson J. Work organization and ergonomics. Geneva: International Labour Office, 1998.

Buchbinder R, Goel V, Bombardier C. Lack of concordance between the ICD-9 classification of soft tissue disorders of the neck and upper limb and chart review diagnosis: one steel mill's experience. American Journal of Industrial Medicine, 1996; 29: 171-182.

Buckle P. Ergonomic stressors related to neurological disorders of the upper limbs. In Bleeker M, ed. Occupational neurology and clinical neurotoxicology. Baltimore: Williams & Wilkins, 1994: 253-267.

Buckle P. Work factors and upper limb disorders. British Medical Journal 1997; 315: 1360-1363.

Burdorf A. Exposure assessment of risk factors for disorders of the back in occupational epidemiology. Scandinavian Journal of Work Environment and Health 1992; 18: 1-9.

Burdorf A, Naaktgeboren B, Post W. Prognostic factors for musculoskeletal sickness absense and return to work among welders and metal workers. Occupational and Environmental Medicine 1998; 55: 490-495.

Burt S. Gender and upper extremity musculoskeletal disorders: Confounding with workplace factors. Proceedings of PRE-MUS-ISEOH '98 3rd International Scientific Conference on Prevention of Work-Related Musculoskeletal Disorders. 21-25 September, Helsinki, Finland, 1998: 236.

Chaffin DB. Localized muscle fatigue - definition and measurement. Journal of Occupational Medicine 1973; 15: 346-354.

Chaffin DB, Andersson GBJ. Occupational Biomechanics. New York: John Wiley & Sons, 1991.

Chiang H-C, Chen S-S, Yu H-S, Ko Y-C. The occurence of carpal tunnel syndrome in frozen food factory employees. Kaohsiung Journal of Medical Science 1990; 6: 73-80.

Chiang H-C, Yin-Ching K, Chen S-S, Hsin-Su Y, Trong-Neng W, Chang P-Y. Prevalence of shoulder and upper-limb disorders among workers in the fish-processing industry. Scandinavian Journal of Work Environment and Health 1993; 19: 126-131.

Colombini D, Occhipinti E, Kilbom Å, Delleman N, Fallentin N, Armstrong T, Santino E. Exposure assessment of upper limb repetitive movements: a consensus document by the IEA Technical Group for WMSDs. Personal Communication, 1998.

Colombini D. An observational method for classifying exposure to repetitive movements of the upper limbs. Ergonomics 1998; 41: 1261-1289.

Colombini D, Occhipinti E, Molteni G, et al. Posture analysis. Ergonomics 1985; 28: 275-284.

Cooper C, Baker PD. Upper limb disorders. Occupational Medicine 1996; 46: 435-437.

Corlett EN. Static muscle loading and the evaluation of posture. In: Wilson JR, Corlett EN, eds. Evaluation of human work, London: Taylor & Francis, 1990: 35-57.

Davies N, Teasdale P. The costs to the British economy of work accidents and work-related ill-health. Sheffield: Health and Safety Executive, 1994.

de Krom MCTFM, Knipschild PG, Kester ADM, Spaans F. Risk factors for carpal tunnel syndrome. American Journal of Epidemiology 1990; 132: 1102-1110.

de Zwart BCH, Broersen J, Van der Beek AJ, Frings-Dresen MHW, Van Dijk FJH. Occupational classification according to work demands: an evaluation study. International Journal of Occupational Medicine and Environmental Health 1997; 10: 283-295.

Devereux JJ, Buckle PW. The impact of work organisation design and management practices upon work related musculoskeletal disorder symptomology. In: Vink P, Koningsveld EAP, Dhondt S, eds. Human factors in organizational design and management - VI, Amsterdam: North-Holland, 1998: 275-279.

Dhondt, S. Time constraints and autonomy at work in the European Union. European Foundation for the Improvement of Living and Working Conditions. Co. Dublin, Ireland. Luxembourg: Office for Official Publications of the European Communities, 1998.

Dhondt S, Houtman ILD. Indicators of working conditions in the European Union. Co. Dublin: European Foundation for the Improvement of Living and Working Conditions, 1997.

Djupsjöbacka M, Johansson H, Bergenheim M, Sjölander P. Influences on the g-muscle-spindle system from contralateral muscle afferents stimulated by KCl and lactic acid. Neuroscience Research 1995; 21: 301-309.

Edwards RHT. Hypothesis of peripheral and central mechanisms underlying occupational muscle pain and injury. European Journal of Applied Physiology 1988; 57: 275-281.

Egan C, Espie B, McGann S, McKenna K, Allen J. Acute effects of vibration on peripheral blood flow in healthy subjects. Occupational and Environmental Medicine 1996; 53: 663-669.

Fransson-Hall C, Kilbom Å. Sensitivity of the hand to surface pressure. Applied Ergonomics 1993; 24: 181-189.

Gelberman F, Herginroeder PT, Hargens AR, Lundborg GN, Akeson WH. The carpal tunnel syndrome: a study of carpal canal pressures. Journal of Bone Joint Surgery 1981; 63A: 380-383.

Goldstein S, Armstrong T, Chaffin D, Matthews L. Analysis of cumulative strain in tendons and tendon sheaths. Journal of Biomechanics 1987; 20: 1-6.

Grieco A, Molteni G, De Vito G, Sias N. Epidemiology of musculoskeletal disorders due to biomechanical overload. Ergonomics 1998; 41: 1253-1260.

Hagberg M. Electromyographic signs of shoulder muscular fatigue in two elevated arm positions. American Journal of Physical Medicine 1981a; 60: 111-121.

Hagberg M. Work load and fatigue in repetitive arm elevations. Ergonomics 1981b; 24: 543-555.

Hagberg M. Occupational musculoskeletal disorders-a new epidemiological challenge? In: Hogstedt C, Reuterwall C, eds. Progress in occupational epidemiology, Elsevier Science Publisher, 1988: 15-26.

Hagberg M, Silverstein BA, Wells RV, Smith MJ, Hendrick HW, Carayon P, Pérusse M.. Work related musculoskeletal disorders: a reference for prevention; Kuorinka I & Forcier L (eds). London: Taylor and Francis, 1995.

Hagberg M, Wegman DH. Prevalence rates and odds ratios of shoulder-neck diseases in different occupational groups. British Journal of Industrial Medicine 1987; 44: 602-610.

Haines HM, Wilson JR. Development of a framework for participatory ergonomics. HSE contract research report 174/1998. Suffolk: HSE Books, 1998.

Hales T, Sauter SL, Peterson MR, Fine LJ, Putz-Anderson V, Schleifer LR, Ochs TT, Bernard BP. Musculoskeletal disorders among visual display terminal users in a telecommunications company. Ergonomics 1994; 37: 1603-1621.

Hansen SM, Jensen PL. Arbeidsmiljö og samfundsekonomi i Norden (Working environment and national economies in the Nordic Countries. Nordic Council of Ministers (Report No. 556), 1993.

Harma MI, Ilmarinen J, Knauth, P, Rutenfranz J, Hanninen O. Physical training intervention in female shift workers: I. The effects of intervention of fitness, fatigue, sleep, and psychosomatic symptoms. Ergonomics 1988; 31: 39-50.

Harms-Ringdahl K, Ekholm J. Intensity and character of pain and muscular activity levels elicited by maintained extreme flexion position of the lower-cervical-upper-thoracic spine. Scandinavian Journal of Rehabilitation Medicine 1986; 18: 117-126.

Harrington JM. Research priorities in occupational medicine: a survey of United Kingdom medical opinion by the Delphi technique. Occupational and Environmental Medicine 1994; 51: 289-294.

Harrington JM, Calvert IA. Research priorities in occupational medicine: a survey of United Kingdom personnel managers. Occupational and Environmental Medicine 1996; 53: 642-644.

Harrington JM, Carter JT, Gompertz D. Surveillance case definitions for work-related upper limb pain syndromes. Occupational and Environmental Medicine 1998; 55: 264-271.

Haselgrave, C. Predicting postures adopted for force exertion: Thesis summary. Clinical Biomechanics 1992; 7: 249-250.

Hägg G. Muscle fibre abnormalities in the upper trapezius muscle related to occupational static load. International Conference in Occupational Disorders of the Upper Extremities, Dec 10-11, Burlingame, California, University of Michigan and the University of California 1998; no page number.

Häkkänen M, Viikari-Juntura E, Takala E-P. Effects of changes in work methods on musculoskeletal load. An intervention study in the trailer assembly. Applied Ergonomics 1997; 28: 99-108.

Health and Safety Commission. Health and safety statistics. Statistical supplement to the 1994-5 annual report. Suffolk, HSE Books, 1995.

Health and Safety Commission. Health and safety statistics 1997/98. Suffolk: HSE Books, 1998.

Helliwell PS. Diagnostic criteria for work-related upper limb disorders. British Journal of Rheumatology 1996; 35: 1195-1196.

Hendrick H. The ergonomics of economics is the economics of ergonomics. Ergonomics SA 1996; 8: 7-16.

Herberts P, Kadefors R, Andersson G, Petersen I. Shoulder pain in industry-an epidemiologic study on welders. Acta Orthopaedica Scandinavica 1981; 52: 299-306.

Herberts P, Kadefors R, Broman H. Arm positioning in manual tasks: an electromyographical study of loacalised muscle fatigue. Ergonomics 1980; 23: 655-665.

Herberts P, Kadefors R, Sigholm G. Shoulder pain and heavy manual labor.

Clin Orthop Relat Res 1984; 191: 166-178.

Hünting W, Läubli T, Grandjean E. Postural and visual loads at VDT workplace: 1. Constrained postures. Ergonomics 1981; 24: 917-931.

Jarvhölm U, Palmerud G, Karlsson D, Herberts P, Kadefors R. Intramuscular pressure and electromyography in four shoulder muscles. Journal of Orthopaedic Research 1990; 9: 609-619.

Jarvhölm U, Palmerud G, Styf J, Herberts P, Kadefors R. Intramuscular pressure in the supraspinatus muscle. Journal of Orthopaedic Research 1988; 6: 230-238.

Johansson H, Sojka P. Pathophysiology mechanisms involved in genesis and spread of muscular tension in occupational muscle pain and in chronic musculoskeletal pain syndromes:a hypothesis. Medical Hypotheses 1991; 35. 196-203.

Jones JR, Hodgson JT, Clegg TA, Elliott RC. Self-reported work-related illness in 1995: results from a household survey. Sheffield: HSE Books, 1998.

Jonsson B. Measurement and evaluation of local muscular strain on the shoulder during constrained work. Journal of Human Ergology 1982; 11: 73-88.

Jonsson B. The static load component in muscle work. European Journal of Applied Physiology 1988; 57: 305-310.

Karasek R. Job demands, job decision latitude and mental strain: implications for job redesign. Administrative Science Quarterly 1979; 24: 285-307.

Karasek R, Theorell T. Healthy work. New York: Basic Books, 1990.

Karhu O, Kansi P, Kuorinka I. Correcting working postures in industry: a practical method for analysis. Applied Ergonomics 1977; 8: 199-201.

Kauppinen T. Assessment of exposure in occupational epidemiology. Scandinavian Journal of Work Environment and Health 1994; 20: 19-29.

Keir PJ, Wells RP. MRI of the carpal tunnel: implications for carpal tunnel syndrome. In: Kumar S, ed. Advances in industrial ergonomics and safety IV., London: Taylor & Francis, 1992: 753-760.

Keyserling WM, Brouwer M, Silverstein BA. Effectivensss of a joint labor management program in controlling awkward postures of the trunk, neck and shoulders. Results of a field study. International Journal of Industrial Ergonomics 1993; 11: 51-65.

Kilbom Å. Repetitive work of the upper extremity: Part II – The scientific basis (knowledge base) for the guide. International Journal of Industrial Ergonomics 1994; 14: 59-86.

Kilbom Å. Prevention of musculoskeletal disorders through standards and guidelines; possibilities and limitations. From Research to Prevention. Managing Occupational and Environmental Health Hazards, People and Work.Research Reports 4, Proceedings of the International Symposium, 20-23 March, 1995, Helsinki, Finland, J.Rantanen, .S.Lehtinen, S.Hernberg et al., 1995; 178-185.

Kilbom Å, Armstrong TJ, Buckle P, Fine LJ, Hagberg M, Haring-Sweeney M, Martin B, Punnett L, Silverstein B, Sjøgaard G, Theorell T, Viikari-Juntura E. Musculoskeletal disorders: Work-related risk factors and prevention. International Journal of Occupational and Environmental Health 1996; 2: 239-246.

Kilbom Å, Persson J, Jonsson BG. Disorders of the cervicobrachial region among female workers in the electronics industry. International Journal of Industrial Ergonomics 1986; 1: 37-47.

Kirwan B, Ainsworth LK. A guide to task analysis. London: Taylor & Francis, 1992.

Last JM. A dictionary of epidemiology. Oxford: Oxford University Press, 1983.

Latko WA, Armstrong TJ, Foulke JA, Herrin GD, Rabourn RA, Ulin SS. Development and evaluation of an observational method for assessing repetition in hand tasks. American Industrial Hygiene Association Journal, 1997; 58: 278-285.

Levine JD. Reflex neuroseptic inflammation. Journal of Neuroscience 1985; 5: 1380-1385.

Li G. and Buckle, P. A practical method for the assessment of work-related musculoskeletal risks - Quick Exposure Check (QEC), Proceedings of the Human Factors and Ergonomics Society 42nd Annual Meeting. 5-9 October, Chicago, Illinois, 1998; 2: 1351-1355.

Li G, Buckle P. Current techniques for assessing physical exposure to work-related musculoskeletal risks, with emphasis on posture-based methods. Ergonomics 1999; 42: 674-695.

Lindström K. Psychosocial criteria for good work organization. Scandinavian Journal of Work Environment and Health 1994; 20: 123-133.

Loeser JD, Melzack R. Pain: an overview. The Lancet 1999; 353: 1607-1609.

Luopajärvi T, Kuorinka I, Virolainen M. Prevalence of tenosynovitis and other injuries of the upper extremities in repetitive work. Scandinavian Journal of Work Environment and Health 1979; 5: 48-55.

Malchaire J, Cock N, Robert AR. Prevalence of musculoskeletal disorders at the wrist as a function of angles, forces, repetitiveness and movement velocities. Scandinavian Journal of Work Environment and Health 1996; 22: 176-181.

Marras WS, Schoenmarklin RW. Wrist motions in industry. Ergonomics 1993; 36: 341-351.

Mathiassen SE, Winkel J. Quantifying variation in physical load using exposure-vs-time data. Ergonomics 1991; 34: 1455-1468.

May DR, Schwoerer CE. Employee health by design: Using employee involvement teams in ergonomic job design. Personnel Psychology 1994; 47: 861-876.

McAtamney L, Corlett EN. RULA: A survey method for the investigation of work-related upper limb disorders. Applied Ergonomics 1993; 24: 91-99.

Melin B, Lundberg U. A biopsychosocial appraoch to work-stress and musculoskeletal disorders. Journal of Psychophysiology 1997; 11: 238-247.

Menoni O, Vimercati C, Panciera D. Clinical trials among worker populations: a model for an anamnestic survey of upper limb pathologies and its practical application methods. Ergonomics 1998; 41: 1312-1321.

Morch M, ed. Yearbook of Nordic statistics. Copenhagen: Nordic Council of Ministers, 1996.

National Research Council. Work-related musculoskeletal disorders: report, workshop summary, and workshop papers. Washington DC: National Research Council, 1999.

NIOSH. Musculoskeletal disorders and workplace factors: a critical review of epidemiologic evidence for work-related musculoskeletal disorders of the neck, upper extremity, and low back. Bernard B (ed.). Cincinnati: DHHS (NIOSH) Publication No. 97-141, 1997.

Nordander C, Ohlsson K, Balogh I, Rylander L, Palsson B, Skerfving S. Fish processing work: the impact of two sex dependent exposure profiles on musculoskeletal health. Occupational and Environmental Medicine 1999; 56: 256-264.

Occhipinti E. OCRA: a concise index for the assessment of exposure to repetitive movements of the upper limbs. Ergonomics 1998; 41: 1290-1311.

Ohlsson K, Attewell R, Skerfving S. Self-reported symptoms in the neck and upper limbs of female assembly workers. Scandinavian Journal of Work Environment and Health 1989; 15: 75-80.

Ohlsson K, Attewell RG, Johnsson B, Ahlm A, Skerfving S. An assessment of neck and upper extremity disorders by questionnaire and clinical examination. Ergonomics 1994; 37: 891-897.

Ohlsson K, Attewell RG, Palsson B, et al. Repetitive industrial work and neck and upper limb disorders in females. American Journal of Industrial Medicine 1995; 27: 731-747.

Ohlsson K, Hansson GA, Balogh I, et al. Disorders of the neck and upper limbs in woman in the fish processing industry. Occupational and Environmental Medicine 1994; 51: 826-832.

Orgel DL, Milliron MJ, Frederick LJ. Musculoskeletal discomfort in grocery express checkstand workers. An ergonomic intervention study. Journal of Occupational Medicine 1992; 34: 815-818.

Otten, F., Bongers, P, Houtman, I. De kans op RSI in Nederland. Gegevens uit het permanent onderzoek leefsituatie, Maandbericht gezondheidsstatistiek (CBS) (The risk of developing RSI in the Netherlands, Data from the Continuous Quality of Life Survey); 11:5-19, 1998.

Paoli, P. The Second European Survey: indicators of working conditions in the European Union. Dublin, The European Foundation for the Improvement of Living and Working Conditions, 1997.

Parenmark G, Engvall B, Malmkvist AK. Ergonomic on-the-job training of assembly workers: arm-neck-shoulder complaints drastically reduced amongst beginners. Applied Ergonomics 1988; 19: 143-146.

Parkes S, Jackson P, Sprigg C, Whybrow A. Organisational interventions to reduce the impact of poor work design. HSE contract research report 196/1998. Suffolk: HSE Books, 1998.

Pedersen J, Sjölander P, Wenngren B, Johansson H. Increased intramuscular concentration of bradykinin increases the static fusimotor drive to muscle spindles in neck muscles of the cat. Pain 1997; 70: 83-91.

Pheasant S. Ergonomics work and health. London: Macmilllan Press, 1991.

Pheasant S. Bodyspace: anthropometry, ergonomics and design. London: Taylor & Francis, 1996.

Pinzke S. A computerised system for analysing working postures in agriculture. International Journal of Industrial Ergonomics 1994; 13: 307-315.

Pyykkö, I. Clinical aspects of the hand-arm vibration syndrome. A review. Scandinavian Journal of Work Environment and Health 1986; 12: 439-447.

Radwin RG, Lavender SA. Work factors, personal factors, and internal loads:Biomechanics of work stressors. Work-related musculoskeletal disorders: report, workshop summary, and workshop papers. National Research Council, Washington D.C: National Academy Press, 1999; 116-151.

Radwin RG, Lin ML, Yen TY. Exposure assessment of biomechanical stress in repetitive manual work using frequency-weighted filters. Ergonomics 1994; 37: 1984-1998.

Rempel D, Dahlin L, Lundborg G. Biological response of peripheral nerves to loading: pathophysiology of nerve compression syndromes and vibration induced neuropathy. Work-related musculoskeletal disorders: report, workshop summary, and workshop papers. National Research Council, Washington D.C: National Academy Press, 1999; 98-115.

Ringelberg JA, Voskamp P. Integrating ergonomic principles into C-Standards for machinery design: TUTB proposals for guidelines. Brussels: European Trade Union Technical Bureau for Health and Safety, 1996.

Rohmert W, Landau K. An new technique for job analysis. London: Taylor & Francis, 1983.

Rubenowitz S. Survey and intervention of ergonomic problems at the workplace. International Journal of Industrial Ergonomics 1997; 19: 271-275.

Sakakibara H, Miyao M, Kondo T, Yamada S, Nakagawa T, Kobayashi F. Relation between overhead work and complaints of pear and apple orchard workers. Ergonomics 1987; 30: 805-815.

Sauter SL, Chapman LJ, Knutson SJ, Anderson HA. Case example of wrist trauma in keyboard use. Applied Ergonomics 1987; 18: 183-186.

Schneider S. Ergonomic intervention has a return on investment of 17 to 1. Applied Occupational and Environmental Hygiene 1998; 13: 212-213.

Schoenmarklin RW, Marras WS. Effects of hand angle and work orientation on hammering: I. Wrist motion and hammering performance. Human Factors 1989; 31: 397-411.

Silverstein B. The prevalence of upper extremity cumulative trauma disorders in industry. PhD Thesis, Ann Arbor: University of Michigan, USA, 1985.

Silverstein BA, Fine LJ, Armstrong TJ. Hand wrist cumulative trauma disorders in industry. British Journal of Industrial Medicine 1986; 43: 779-784.

Sinclair MA. Subjective assessment. In: Wilson JR, Corlett EN, eds. Evaluation of human work, London: Taylor & Francis, 1990: 58-88.

Sjøgaard, G. Work-induced muscle fatigue and its relation to muscle pain. Copenhagen: National Institute of Occupational Health, 1990.

Sluiter, J. K., Visser, B., and Frings, Dresen MHW. Concept guidelines for diagnosing work-related musculoskeletal disorders: the upper extremity. Coronel Institute of Occupational and Environmental Health, Amsterdam Medical Center, University of Amsterdam, The Netherlands, 1998.

Smith EM, Sonstegard D, Anderson W. Carpal tunnel syndrome: contribution of flexor tendons. Arch Phys Med Rehab 1977; 58: 379-385.

Smith MJ, Karsh B-T, Conway FT, Cohen WJ, James CA, Morgan J, Sanders K, Zehel D. Effects of a split keyboard design and wrist rest on performance, posture, and comfort. Human Factors 1998; 40: 324-336.

Smith MJ, Karsh B-T, Moro BP. A review of research on interventions to control musculoskeletal disorders. Work-related musculoskeletal disorders: report, workshop summary, and workshop papers. Washington DC: National Research Council, 1999; 200-229.

Smith MJ, Carayon P. Work organization, stress, and cumulative trauma disorders. In: Moon SD, Sauter SL, eds. Beyond biomechanics: Psychosocial aspects of musculoskeletal disorders in office work. London: Taylor & Francis, 1996: 23-42.

Statistics Sweden. Statistical yearbook of Sweden. Stockholm: Statistics Sweden, 1997.

Strömberg T, Dahlin LB, Brun A, Lundborg G. Structural nerve changes at wrist level in workers exposed to vibration. Occupational and Environmental Medicine, 1997; 54: 307-311.

Sundelin G, Hagberg M. Effects of exposure to excessive draughts on myoelectric activity in shoulder muscles. Journal of Electromyographic Kinesiology 1992; 2: 36-41.

Theorell T. The possible mechanisms behind the relationship between the demand-control-support model and disorders of the locomotor system. In Moon SD & Sauter SL, eds. Beyond biomechanics. Psychosocial aspects of musculoskeletal disorders in office work. London: Taylor and Francis, 1996: 65-73.

Toomingas, A. Methods for evaluating work-related musculoskeletal neck and upper-extremity disorders in epidemiological studies. Arbete Och Hälsa Vetenskaplig Skriftserie 1998:6, Arbetslivinstitutet (National Institute for Working Life), 1998.

Tozzi, G. The ETUC campaign on MSD. Unpublished. Brussels: The European Trade Union Confederation, 1999.

Tulga MK, Sheridan TB. Dynamic decisions and workload in multi-task supervisory control. IEEE transactions on systems, man and cybernetics 1980, SMC-10: 217-232.

TUTB. Musculoskeletal disorders: a European prevention strategy. Newsletter of the European Trade Union Technical Bureau for Health and Safety, Brussels. No.4, November 1996.

TUTB. The working environment in the European Union: the difficult transistion from law to practice. Newsletter of the European Trade Union Technical Bureau for Health and Safety, Brussels. No 8, March 1998.

Vahtera J, Kivimäki M, Pentti J. Effect of organisational downsizing on health of employees. The Lancet 1997; 350: 1124-1128.

Van der Beek AJ, Frings-Dresen MHW. Assessment of mechanical exposure in ergonomic epidemiology. Occupational and Environmental Medicine 1998; 291-299.

Van der Beek AJ, Frings-Dresen MHW, Van Dijk FJH, Houtman ILD. Priorities in occupational health research: a Delphi study in the Netherlands. Occupational and Environmental Medicine 1997; 54: 504-510.

Veiersted KB, Westgaard RH, Andersen P. Pattern of muscle activity during stereotyped work and its relation to muscle pain. International Archives on Occupational and Environmental Health 1990; 62: 31-41.

Veiersted KB, Westgaard RH, Andersen P. Electromyographic evaluation of muscular work pattern as a predictor of trapezius myalgia. Scandinavian Journal of Work Environment and Health 1993; 19: 284-290.

Viikari-Juntura E. The scientific basis for making guidelines and standards to prevent work-related musculoskeletal disorders. Ergonomics 1997; 40: 1097-1117.

Viikari-Juntura E, Silverstein B. Role of physical load factors in the carpal tunnel syndrome. Scandinavian Journal of Work Environment and Health 1999; 25: 163-185.

Vincent MJ, Tipton MJ. The effects of cold immersion and hand protection on grip strength. Aviation, Space, and Environmental Medicine 1988; 59: 738-741.

Waersted M, Westgaard RH. Attention-related muscle activity in different body regions during VDU work with minimal physical activity. Ergonomics 1996; 39: 661-676.

Waris P, Kuorinka I, Kurppa K, Luopajarvi T, Virolainen M, Pesonen K, Nummi J, Kukkonen R. Epidemiologic screening of occupational neck and upper limb disorders: methods and criteria. Scandinavian Journal of Work Environment and Health 1979; 5: 25-38.

Waters TR, Putz-Anderson V, Garg A, Fine LJ. Revised NIOSH equation for the design and evaluation of manual lifting tasks. Ergonomics 1993; 36: 749-776.

Wenngren B, Pedersen J, Sjölander P, Bergenheim M, Johansson H. Bradykinin and muscle stretch alter contralateral cat neck muscle spindle output. Neuroscience Research 1998; 32: 119-129.

Westgaard RH, Winkel J. Guidelines for occupational musculoskeletal load as a basis for intervention: a critical review. Applied Ergonomics 1996, 27: 79-88.

Westgaard RH, Winkel J. Review article: Ergonomic intervention research for improved musculoskeletal health: a critical review. International Journal of Industrial Ergonomics 1997; 20: 463-500

Wiker SF, Chaffin DB, Langolf GD. Shoulder posture and localized muscle fatigue and discomfort. Ergonomics 1989; 32: 211-237.

Wiktorin C, Mortimer M, Ekenvall L, Kilbom Å, Wigaeus-Hjelm E. HARBO, a simple computer-aided observation method for recording work postures. Scandinavian Journal of Work Environment and Health 1995; 21: 440-449.

Wilson JR. A framework and a context for ergonomics methodology. In: Wilson JR, Corlett EN, eds. Evaluation of human work. London: Taylor & Francis, 1990: 1-24.

Winkel J, Mathiassen SE. Assessment of physical work load in epidemiologic studies: concepts, issues and operational considerations. Ergonomics, 1994; 37: 979-988.

Winkel J, Westgaard RH. Occupational and individual risk factors for shoulder-neck complaints: Part II-The scientific basis (literature review) for the guide. International Journal of Industrial Ergonomics 1992; 10: 85-104.

World Health Organization (WHO)-Identification and control of work related diseases. Technical report: no 174, 1985.

Zwerling C, Daltroy LH, Fine LJ, Johnston JJ, Melius J, Silverstein BA. Design and conduct of occupational injury intervention studies: a review of evaluation strategies. American Journal of Industrial Medicine 1997; 32: 164-179

CEN, ISO and national legislation and guidance

Council of the European Union (1994). Amended proposal for a council directive on the minimum health and safety requirements regarding the exposure of workers to the risks arising from physical agents – individual directive in relation to Article 16 of the Directive 89/391/EEC. Off J Eur Communities 94/C230/03: C230/3-29.

Council Directive 93/104/EC of 23rd November 1993 concerning aspects of the organization of working time. Official journal NO.L 307, 13/12/1993 P. 0018-0024.

Council Directive 89/391/EEC of 12 June 1989 on the introduction of measures to enourage improvements in the safety and health of workers at work. Official journal No. L 183, 29/06/1989 P. 0001-0008.

Mechanical vibration – Guide to the health effects of vibration on the human body CEN CR 12349:1996 E.

Safety of machinery – Ergonomic design principles – Part I: Terminology and general principles EN 614-1: 1995

Hand-arm vibration – Guidelines for vibration hazards reduction – Part 1: engineering methods by design of machinery CR 1030-1: 1995.

Mechanical vibration – Guidelines for the measurement and assessment of human exposure to hand-transmitted vibration ENV 25349: 1992 (ISO 5349: 1986).

Ergonomics for the Prevention of Musculoskeletal Disorders. Statute Book of the Swedish National Board of Occupational Safety and Health, AFS 1998:1. Stockholm Elanders:Gotab, Sweden 1998.

Committee Draft CEN/TC 231 N 294 (1998)

ISO/CD 5349-2 (1999)

Ergonomic principles related to mental work-load – General terms and definitions. International Standard ISO 10075:1991 E.

Ergonomic principles related to mental work-load – Part 2: Design Principles. International Standard ISO 10075-2: 1996 E.

Safety of machinery - Human physical performance - Part 4: Evaluation of working postures in relation to machinery prEN 1005-4: 1998.

Safety of machinery - Human physical performance - Part 3: Recommended force limits for machinery operation prEN 10005-3: 1998.

Safety of machinery – Human physical performance - Part 2: Manual handling of objects associated with machinery prEN 1005-2: 1998.

Safety of machinery – Human physical performance - Part 1: Terms and definitions prEN 1005-1: 1998.

RESEARCH

11.

APPENDICES

A.1

APPENDIX 1.

PROJECT ORGANISATION

Steering committee

Dr. M. Aaltonen, Project Manager, Research
European Agency for Safety and Health at Work
Gran Via, 33
E-48009 Bilbao SPAIN

Dr. G. Aresini, Dr. C. Martin, Dr. F. Alvarez
European Commission, Directorate-General V
Employment, Industrial Relations and Social Affairs
Public health and safety and at work
Health, safety and hygiene at work
Rue Alcide de Gasperi
EUFO 4270
L-2920 Luxembourg

Prof. P. Buckle, (project leader), **Dr. J. Devereux** (technical secretariat)

Robens Centre for Health Ergonomics

European Institute of Health & Medical Sciences

University of Surrey, Guildford, Surrey, U.K. GU2 5XH

Committee of scientific experts

Professor Tom Armstrong, Centre for Ergonomics, University of Michigan, Ann Arbor, Michigan 48109-2029, U.S.A.

Dr. Massimo Bovenzi, Institute of Occupational Health, University of Trieste, Centro Tumori, I-34129 Trieste, Italy.

Professor Asa Kilbom, Centre for Ergonomics, National Institute of Working Life, S-171 84 Solna, Sweden.

Professor Monique H.W. Frings-Dresen, Coronel Institute for Occupational and Environmental Health, Academic Medical Center, Meibergdreef 15, 1105 AZ Amsterdam, The Netherlands

Dr. Larry Fine, National Institute of Occupational Safety and Health, Columbia Parkway, Cincinnatti, Ohio, U.S.A.

Dr. Paulien Bongers TNO Work and Employment, Polaris Avenue 151, 2132 JJ Hoofddorp, The Netherlands

Professor Peter Buckle and **Dr. Jason Devereux,** Robens Centre for Health Ergonomics, European Institute of Health & Medical Sciences, University of Surrey, Guildford, Surrey, U.K. GU2 5XH

A.2

APPENDIX 2.

SUMMARY OF CONSULTATION

These included meetings with representatives from the National Institute for Working Life, Sweden; the University of Gothenburg, Sweden; the University of Milan, Italy; the Health and Safety Executive in the UK, consultation with trade union bodies, NIOSH in the United States, consultation with DG V and some dissemination of key information to appropriate member states.

Meetings have been held with the Trade Union Technical Bureau for Health and Safety in Brussels, Belgium and the French employer's federation CNPF.

There has also been liaison with the Coronel Institute, Amsterdam who are developing diagnostic criteria for upper limb disorders and with TNO Work and Employment, Hoofddorp, who are involved with other European research projects investigating work-related neck and upper limb disorders under the SAFE programme.

The approach has been presented and/or discussed at the following meetings:

- Organisational Design and Management 6 , The Hague, Netherlands, August 1998

- PREMUS-ISEOH, Helsinki, Finland, September, 1998

- Occupational Disorders of the Upper Extremities, Universities of Berkeley, UCLA and University of Michigan, December 1998

- New Perspectives in Occupational Medicine Meeting, School of Public Policy, University College London, March 1999

- Contemporary Ergonomics, Ergonomics Society Annual Conference, University of Leicester, England, April 1999

- RSI, Law and Medicine Trades Union Congress (TUC) Meeting , London, England, April 1999

These conferences provided a forum for discussion and feedback on the approach taken.

The special consultation process was carried out in the summer of 1999 by sending the manuscript to the members of the Thematic Network Group on Research - Work and Health, DGV, European social partners (ETUC, UNICE) and other international experts on the topic.

A.3

APPENDIX 3.

LITERATURE SEARCH TERMS

AND DATABASES

Databases searched

BIDS-ONLINE
NIOSHTIC
MEDLINE
HSELINE
CISDOC
OSH-CD

Keywords for search

MESH terms

Arm-injuries-epidemiology
Arm-injuries-etiology
Cumulative-trauma-disorders-epidemiology
Cumulative-trauma-disorders-etiology
Hand-injuries-epidemiology
Hand-injuries-etiology
Cumulative-trauma-disorders-prevention & control
Musculoskeletal diseases

Cumulative trauma disorders
Musculoskeletal system disorders

Non-MESH terms

RSI or repetitive strain injur*
WRULD*
work related upper limb disorder*
WRUED*
work related upper extremity disorder*
repetition strain injury
epidemiology
etiology
cumulative trauma disorders
neck
tension neck syndrome
shoulder
rotator cuff
elbow
epicondylitis
tendinitis
tenosynovitis
carpal tunnel
de Quervain's
nerve entrapment syndrome
vibration
hand arm vibration syndrome
vibration white finger
Raynaud's phenomenon
Dupuytren's contracture
Trigger finger
Cubital tunnel syndrome
Guyon canal syndrome
Pronator teres syndrome
Radial tunnel syndrome
Thoracic outlet syndrome
Cervical syndrome
Digital neuritis
Hypothenar hammer syndrome

Adverse mechanical tension
Myotherapy –trigger points
Fibrositis
Myofascial syndrome
Chronic pain
myalgia
Reviews
Occupational Diseases physiopathology
Pain physiopathology
mechanisms
Myofascial Pain Syndromes etiology
Myofascial Pain Syndromes physiopathology
Neck physiopathology
Cumulative Trauma Disorders complications

Shoulder physiology
Fatigue physiopathology
Microcirculation physiology
Neck physiopathology
Soft Tissue Injuries physiopathology
Pain physiopathology
chronic pain
Muscles physiopathology
Intervention
Review

Note:

Additional Mesh and Non-mesh terms have been included during the iterative literature search process.

A.4

APPENDIX 4.

SUMMARY TABLES OF

POSTURAL RISK FACTORS

(Hagberg et al., 1995)

Postural risk factors reported in the literature for the shoulders.

Risk factor	Results: Outcome and details	References
More than 60° abduction or flexion for more than 1 hour/day	Acute shoulder and neck pain	Bjelle et al., 1981
Less than 15° median upper arm flexion and 10° abduction for continuous work with low loads	Increased sick leave due to musculoskeletal problems	Aaras et al., 1988
Abduction greater than 30°	Rapid fatigue at greater abduction angles	Chaffin, 1973
Abduction greater than 45°	Rapid fatigue at 90°	Herberts et al., 1980

Risk factor	Results: Outcome and details	References
Abduction greater than 100	Hyperabduction syndrome with compression of blood vessels	Beyer and Wright, 1951
Shoulder forward flexion of 30°, Abduction greater than 30°	Impairment of blood flow in the supraspinatus muscle	Järvholm et al., 1988 Järvholm et al., 1990
Hands no greater than 35° above shoulder level	Onset of local muscle fatigue	Wiker et al., 1989
Upper arm flexion or abduction of 90°	Electromyographic signs of local muscle fatigue in less than one minute	Hagberg, 1981a
Hands at or above shoulder height	Tendinitis and other shoulder disorders	Bjelle et al., 1979 Herberts et al., 1981 Herberts et al., 1984
Repetitive shoulder flexion	Acute fatigue	Hagberg, 1981b
Repetitive shoulder abduction or flexion	Neck/shoulder symptoms negatively related to movement rate	Kilbom et al., 1986
Postures invoking static shoulder loads	Tendinitis and other shoulder disorders	Luopajärvi et al., 1979
Arm elevation	Pain	Sakakibara et al., 1987
Shoulder elevation	Neck/shoulder symptoms	Jonsson et al., 1988
Shoulder elevation and upper arm abduction	Neck/shoulder symptoms	Kilbom et al., 1986

Risk factor	Results: Outcome and details	References
Abduction and forward flexion invoking static shoulder loads	Shoulder pain and sick leave due to musculoskeletal problems	Aarås and Westgaard, 1987 Aarås et al., 1987
Overhead reaching and lifting	Pain	Bateman, 1983

Postural risk factors reported in the literature for the neck.

Risk factor	Results: Outcome and details	References
Static flexion	No pain in the neck or EMG changes at 15° flexion for 6 hours. At 30° flexion, it took 300 mins for severe pain to occur. At 60° flexion, the corresponding time was 120 mins	Chaffin, 1973
Flexion	Head inclination more than 56° pain and tenderness in medical examination in 2/3 of the cases	Hünting et al., 1981
Dynamic flexion	Median flexion of between 19° and 39° resulted in low sick leave due to musculoskeletal problems	Aaras et al., 1988
Maximum static flexion	Rapid development of pain at end of range of motion	Harms-Ringdahl and Ekholm, 1986

Postural risk factors reported in the literature for the hand and wrist.

Risk factor	Results: Outcome and details	References
Wrist flexion	CTS. Exposure of 20-40 hours/week	de Krom et al., 1990
Wrist flexion	Increased median nerve stresses (pressure)	Smith et al., 1977
Wrist flexion	Increased finger flexor muscle activation for grasping	Moore et al., 1991
Wrist flexion	Median nerve compression by flexor tendons	Armstrong and Chaffin, 1978; Moore et al., 1991
Wrist extension	Median nerve compression by flexor tendons	Keir and Wells, 1992
Wrist extension	CTS. Exposure of 20-40 hours/week	de Krom et al., 1990
Wrist extension	Increased intra-carpal tunnel pressure for extreme extension of 90	Gelberman et al., 1981
Wrist extension	Increased median nerve stresses for extension of 45-90	Smith et al., 1977
Wrist ulnar deviation	Exposure response effect found: if deviation greater than 20 increased pain and pathological findings	Hunting et al., 1981

Risk factor	Results: Outcome and details	References
Deviated wrist positions	Workers with carpal tunnel syndrome used these postures more often	Armstrong and Chaffin 1979
Hand manipulations	More than 500-2000 manipulations per hour led to tenosynovitis	Hammer 1934
Wrist motion	1276 flexion extension motions lead to fatigue	Bishu et al., 1990
Wrist motion	Higher wrist accelerations and velocities in high-risk wrist WMSD jobs	Marras and Schoenmarkin 1993

A.5

APPENDIX 5.

ANNEX I

OF THE MINIMUM HEALTH

AND SAFETY REQUIREMENTS

FOR THE MANUAL HANDLING

OF LOADS

Council Directive 90/269/EEC of 29 May 1990 on the minimum health and safety requirements for the manual handling of loads where there is a risk particularly of back injury to workers (fourth individual Directive within the meaning of Article 16 (1) of Directive 89/391/EEC)

Official journal NO. L 156 , 21/06/1990 P. 0009 - 0013

ANNEX I

(*) REFERENCE FACTORS (Article 3 (2), Article 4 (a) and (b) and Article 6 (2))

1. Characteristics of the load

The manual handling of a load may present a risk particularly of back injury if it is:
- too heavy or too large,
- unwieldy or difficult to grasp,
- unstable or has contents likely to shift,
- positioned in a manner requiring it to be held or manipulated at a distance from the trunk, or with a bending or twisting of the trunk,
- likely, because of its contours and/or consistency, to result in injury to workers, particularly in the event of a collision.

2. Physical effort required

A physical effort may present a risk particularly of back injury if it is:
  too strenuous,
- only achieved by a twisting movement of the trunk,
- likely to result in a sudden movement of the load,
- made with the body in an unstable posture.

3. Characteristics of the working environment

The characteristics of the work environment may increase a risk particularly of back injury if:
- there is not enough room, in particular vertically, to carry out the activity,
- the floor is uneven, thus presenting tripping hazards, or is slippery in relation to the worker's footwear,

- the place of work or the working environment prevents the handling of loads at a safe height or with good posture by the worker,
- there are variations in the level of the floor or the working surface, requiring the load to be manipulated on different levels,
- the floor or foot rest is unstable,
- the temperature, humidity or ventilation is unsuitable.

4. Requirements of the activity

The activity may present a risk particularly of back injury if it entails one or more of the following requirements:
- over-frequent or over-prolonged physical effort involving in particular the spine,
- an insufficient bodily rest or recovery period,
- excessive lifting, lowering or carrying distances,
- a rate of work imposed by a process which cannot be altered by the worker.

(*) With a view to making a multi-factor analysis, reference may be made simultaneously to the various factors listed in Annexes I and II.

ANNEX II

(*) INDIVIDUAL RISK FACTORS (Articles 5 and 6 (2)) The worker may be at risk if he/she:

- is physically unsuited to carry out the task in question,
- is wearing unsuitable clothing, footwear or other personal effects,
- does not have adequate or appropriate knowledge or training.

(*) With a view to multi-factor analysis, reference may be made simultaneously to the various factors listed in Annexes I and II.

European Agency for Safety and Health at Work

Work-related neck and upper limb musculoskeletal disorders

Luxembourg: Office for Official Publications of the European Communities

1999 — 114 pp. — 14.8 x 21 cm

ISBN 92-828-8174-1

Price (excluding VAT) in Luxembourg: EUR 7